ALSO BY NARGISSE BENKABBOU

Casablanca: My Moroccan Food

MADAQ

Chez Ali
N 14
26

MADAQ

simple and delicious everyday recipes with the flavors of **MOROCCO**

NARGISSE BENKABBOU

ALFRED A. KNOPF, NEW YORK, 2026

A BORZOI BOOK
FIRST HARDCOVER EDITION
PUBLISHED BY ALFRED A. KNOPF 2026

Published by Alfred A. Knopf, a division of Penguin Random House LLC, 1745 Broadway, New York, NY 10019.

Knopf, Borzoi Books, and the colophon are registered trademarks of Penguin Random House LLC.
Library of Congress Cataloging-in-Publication Data
Names: Benkabbou, Nargisse, author.
Title: Madaq: simple and delicious everyday recipes with the flavors of
Morocco / Nargisse Benkabbou.
Description: First edition. | New York: Alfred A. Knopf, 2026.
Identifiers: LCCN 2024052851 | ISBN 9780593801604 (hardcover) | ISBN
9780593801611 (ebook)
Subjects: LCSH: Cooking, Moroccan. | LCGFT: Cookbooks.
Classification: LCC TX725.M8 B448 2026 |
DDC 641.5964—dc23/eng/20241205
LC record available at https://lccn.loc.gov/2024052851

Some of the recipes in this book may include raw eggs, meat, or fish. When these foods are consumed raw, there is always the risk that bacteria, which is killed by proper cooking, may be present. For this reason, when serving these foods raw, always buy certified salmonella-free eggs and the freshest meat and fish available from a reliable grocer, storing them in the refrigerator until they are served. Because of the health risks associated with the consumption of bacteria that can be present in raw eggs, meat, and fish, these foods should not be consumed by infants, small children, pregnant women, the elderly, or any persons who may be immunocompromised. The author and publisher expressly disclaim responsibility for any adverse effects that may result from the use or application of the recipes and information contained in this book.

penguinrandomhouse.com | aaknopf.com

Printed in China

1 2 3 4 5 6 7 8 9 10

The authorized representative in the EU for product safety and compliance is Penguin Random House Ireland, Morrison Chambers, 32 Nassau Street, Dublin D02 YH68, Ireland, https://eu-contact.penguin.ie.

CAFE
BY MACHI MOCHKIL

TO PAPA,

FOR GIVING ME

HIS ZEST FOR LIFE

AND LOVE FOR

GOOD FOOD

CONTENTS

MADAQ

INTRODUCTION

The word "madaq" means "flavor" in Moroccan Arabic. It comes from the word قاذم, pronounced /mæ-θq/ or "mathaq" in classical Arabic, which also translates as "flavor" or "taste." Flavor is an essential part of our everyday lives; it's what truly ignites our passion for food. It holds a special place in the way we eat, and it's the magic "ingredient" that transforms a meal into a memorable experience.

Our perception of flavor isn't just swayed by the complexity of its dish, its elegance, or its presentation. When we really enjoy a meal, it's because it tastes delicious. We find ourselves going back for seconds when we enjoy a dish that is full of flavor and simply irresistible. The art of balancing flavors—achieving just the right amount of saltiness, sweetness, or acidity, for example—is often what takes a dish of any kind to the next level.

Flavorful foods leave an indelible mark on your palate, an unforgettable taste memory. Think of the sweet, slightly tart allure of raspberries; the perfection of sun-ripened tomatoes; the explosion of tangy sweetness in every bite of a ripe nectarine. And then recall memories of a slow-cooked hearty stew; a fragrant, spicy vegetable curry; or an exquisite rich, dark chocolate

cake. Those are the dishes we crave and hold close, the ones that capture our attention and keep it; it's as if they hold a special key to our taste buds, and once they turn it, there's no going back.

I can remember that even at a young age I embraced the wonders of Moroccan cooking. Moroccan food seemed to represent a symphony of flavors, an art mastered only by my mom and aunties. I'd watch them in the kitchen peeling, chopping, laughing, cooking, and tasting—it all seemed beautiful and almost effortless. And it fueled my curiosity as well, eventually inspiring me to immerse myself in the world of authentic Moroccan cuisine and its signature flavors.

If there's one thing that sets Moroccan cuisine apart from so many others, it's the unmistakable pursuit of bold flavors in every dish, what we know as madaq. If you're at all familiar with traditional Moroccan cooking, you know that it doesn't rely on extravagant ingredients or complex techniques. Instead, it celebrates the beauty of simplicity. At serving time, all the dishes are placed family-style in the center of the table, inviting everyone to help themselves. When making a classic tagine, one of the most important ingredients is time. Crafting one is an exercise in patience, allowing all the spices to steep and meld together in order to bring out all their aromas. This simple approach to cooking highlights how everyday ingredients can be effortlessly transformed into special meals filled with depth and complexity.

I wrote this cookbook to show you how to bring bold Moroccan flavors into your own kitchen—with simple ingredients and straightforward techniques. With *Madaq*, I hope to take you on a journey where new flavors feel exciting, approachable, and always worth sharing.

MY STORY

My parents emigrated from Fez, Morocco, to Brussels in the 1970s. Like many immigrants, they didn't really know how long they would spend in their new country. Morocco was their place of birth, and they were planning to go back there eventually. Being the child of immigrants meant that the culture and the environment I grew up in was the culture of my parents' birthplace.

Moroccan culture is a rich blend of Arab and Amazigh (Berber) cultures. The blend of these two historically singular cultures is powerful and complex. It's colorful in many ways, pleasantly loud, and deliciously generous. Moroccans place a strong emphasis on ceremony, with rituals and cooking taking center stage at every family gathering, celebration, or holiday. In fact, we seem to have a special dish for every occasion.

Both my parents are food obsessed, and they used food as a way to anchor us to our Moroccan heritage. So, even though we were in the heart of Brussels, our dining table was really a little piece of Morocco. Mornings started with a breakfast spread that transported us straight back to Fez: fried eggs accompanied by khlii, a savory preserved meat akin to beef jerky; m'semen, a delectable, layered pan-fried bread reminiscent of paratha; and baghrir, semolina pancakes drenched in a syrup of honey, fragrant orange blossom water, and melted butter. For dinner, we'd usually enjoy a tagine or grilled fish, chicken, or meat, served with an assortment of salads and dips seasoned with extra-virgin olive oil and aromatic spices. And there was always an abundance of homemade Moroccan breads of one type or another to round out the meal. Even school lunches were all about tagine leftovers, which my mom magically turned into sandwiches served on French baguettes.

I left my parents' home for Paris when I was twenty-two to pursue my education there. I often look back on that time as my true introduction to adult life. I was living on my own for the first time, responsible for my own home, and I started preparing my own meals. During those initial weeks in Paris, I became part of a lovely group of new friends, and we established a tradition of hosting weekly dinner parties. Each member of our diverse group came from a different part of the world, and we took turns preparing meals from our own countries. When my first time to cook finally came, though, it dawned on me that I had never made a Moroccan meal entirely on my own. So I did what any self-respecting adult would do: I called my mom and asked her dozens of questions to make sure this first meal would be a success. The dinner went so well that it ignited my passion for cooking and feeding others.

After two years in Paris, I moved to London to study public policy. But my passion for cooking Moroccan food continued to burn brightly, and I began to take great pleasure in sharing flavorful meals with friends and classmates. Back then, though, the idea of a career in food hadn't crossed my mind—I was just following the expected path and focusing on my education. But London, with its incredible food scene, had a different plan for me. It was there that I discovered contemporary cooking, fusion food, and the most diverse range of restaurants and cuisines imaginable. I fell head over heels with the concept of creating something entirely new by taking a beloved cuisine and giving it a contemporary twist, making it more accessible in the process.

So, after a few years, I made the bold decision to leave my job and dive headfirst into cooking school. My journey from novice cook to food professional took time, time for me to find my rhythm, culinary identity, and my personal style, whether as a chef or food writer. But what kept me going was my belief that it was my mission to share the rich heritage of my country through its food, to show that Moroccan food and culture go beyond stereotypes like greasy tagines and overly sweet cookies. And today, whether I'm creating a new dish for my restaurant or developing a recipe for the home cook, my mission remains the same: sharing the essence of Moroccan cuisine with others. With that same goal I wrote this cookbook, which is all about celebrating the heart and soul of Moroccan food.

MODERN MOROCCO

As the child of immigrants, and an immigrant myself, though I've lived in the UK for more than fifteen years, I have sometimes found myself struggling to define my own identity. I've always felt a deep connection to my Moroccan heritage, certainly, but there are times where I haven't felt entirely Moroccan in Morocco, not really Belgian in Belgium, and not yet a total Londoner in the UK. In our modern era, defining one's identity is a tricky process, one that extends beyond the traditional markers of nationality and geographical location. Rather, it's an intricate mix of cultures, experiences, and other outside influences.

Still, I've always felt that my prominent identity is Moroccan. I take immense pride in my heritage, and witnessing the country's evolution and increasing openness over the last decade has brought me a lot of joy. Morocco's commitment to embracing tourism and nurturing a thriving economy is a source of optimism for me, and the flourishing multiculturalism there today is a testament to our nation's welcoming spirit.

The modernization of the country has made it easier for visitors to access the wonders of Morocco. Our country's diverse landscapes, from the majestic Atlas Mountains to the seemingly endless Sahara Desert to the picturesque coastal cities, are still treasures waiting to be explored, and it warms my heart to see that more and more travelers from around the world are discovering the beauty and the magic of my country. What I also find heartening is how Morocco is slowly becoming a more multicultural society, whether for Moroccan emigrants now returning home or for non-Moroccan expats. The influx of tourists as well as of expatriates has enriched our communities with a diversity of skills, cultures, languages, and perspectives, and promoted an environment of openness and tolerance.

In the midst of these transformations, Morocco remains a land of enchantment, where ancient history meets modern progress, and where the warmth of our people is a constant reminder of our shared humanity. As Morocco continues to attract more people to its shores, Moroccan culture and food are gradually gaining recognition worldwide. As a chef, I can't help but applaud the increasing presence of Moroccan cuisine around the globe. When I moved to London all those years ago, it was a struggle to find ingredients like preserved lemons, ras el hanout, or harissa, but today Moroccan flavors and ingredients have found their place on international tables.

MOROCCAN CUISINE OVER TIME

Moroccan cuisine is the result of a melting pot of cultures, where each historical presence in the royal kingdom has left its mark. The country's culinary legacy reflects its enviable geographical position as a meeting point for various civilizations, where a blend of trade routes and historical conquests came together to create a unique culinary tradition.

The earliest influences on Moroccan cuisine can be traced back to the indigenous Amazigh, also known as Berbers, who have inhabited North Africa for thousands of years. Their culinary heritage revolved around staples like couscous, preserved meat, and dairy products, which continue to be integral to our cuisine. The Berbers also introduced the tagine pot and are in fact responsible for the techniques used to make the dish.

The Arab arrival in the seventh century brought exotic spices such as cumin, coriander, and cinnamon, introducing a complexity of seasoning to the cuisine that is still evident today. The Moors, Muslims based

primarily on the Iberian Peninsula during the eighth century, also had a strong influence. Their legacy included the widespread cultivation of olive trees, for their fruit and oil, along with citrus groves and other fruit orchards across Morocco.

In the late fifteenth century, following their displacement from Spain and Portugal, Jews and Muslims from Iberia found refuge in Morocco. They brought with them culinary knowledge and techniques ranging from delicate pastry-making and bread traditions to slow-simmered stews and preservation methods, all of which became woven into Morocco's broader culinary identity.

The country's location on the Mediterranean coast connected it to the maritime trade routes, in turn introducing seafood into the cuisine. That Mediterranean influence can be seen in dishes such as seafood bastilla and fish kefta "meatball" tagine, two specialties from the north of Morocco. The country's position as a trading hub along the trans-Saharan caravan routes brought spices like saffron and ginger, further enriching the Moroccan spice palate. In 1912, the French colonization of Morocco opened a new culinary chapter. The French presence, which introduced a café culture, an appreciation of fine wines, and the art of patisserie, infused the cuisine with a cosmopolitan flair that persists to this day.

The imperial dynasties that ruled Morocco over the centuries, from the Almoravids to the Alaouites, each left their own culinary legacy. The royal kitchens, often staffed by renowned chefs, played a pivotal role in refining and innovating Moroccan cuisine, leading to the creation of impressive dishes like chicken bastilla and lamb mechoui.

Today Morocco's cuisine serves as a vibrant testament to the dynamic interplay of cultures, trade, and dynasties that have defined the country's identity over the centuries. These influences are very much reflected in the way I cook and develop recipes, but my approach has also been shaped by my own personal culinary experiences. As a result, you will find some recipes here, like the Ras el Hanout Mushroom Tacos, which were inspired by Mexican cooking, or the Kefta and Kale Couscous Bowls, with their hints of Lao and Thai influence, that are by no means traditional Moroccan dishes. Their core flavors, however, remain undeniably Moroccan.

MOROCCAN FOOD

Moroccan cuisine is diverse, vibrant, aromatic, and full of flavor—the madaq that leaves an indelible impression. The country is famous for its tagines, those iconic stews made with succulent meat, poultry, or fish cooked in a fragrant sauce, that are named for the earthenware pots they are traditionally cooked in. Other well-known dishes include scented couscous, aromatic salads, and fragrant roasts seasoned with ras el hanout, the classic spice blend. Chermoula, the marinade made with herbs, spices, and fresh lemon juice, is another hallmark of the cuisine. As for sweets, there are many types of almond pastries, coated in honey and drizzled with orange blossom water, sweet flatbreads, and, of course, Morocco's iconic mint tea.

Yet beyond these more familiar dishes, there is a world of culinary gems waiting to be more widely discovered: dishes like t'faya, a sweet and spicy condiment of caramelized onion and raisin; zaalouk, a smoky eggplant and tomato dip; berkoukes, a traditional Berber dish made with small pasta pearls. Many of these are surprisingly simple to prepare. With *Madaq*, then, I am excited to be able to allow you to discover the delicious flavors of Moroccan cuisine, and I hope the recipes in this cookbook leave your taste buds just as happy as they always leave mine.

TOOLS TO DEVELOP MADAQ

Cooking, for many of us, isn't just about preparing food to satisfy our hunger—it can be a form of meditation and discovery. As we chop, season, and simmer, we delight in the wonderful smells that fill our kitchens. Almost every ingredient or technique has a story to tell and represents a tradition or a culture, while the cooking process itself feels like a calming ritual. I think one of the many reasons behind my decision to become a chef was to be able to appreciate the stillness that is often present in cooking.

But while I love making time to slow down and truly enjoy the process of cooking at home, there are many days when I am desperate for quick and effortless ways to put food on the table for my family. If this sounds familiar, know that you're not alone. The truth is, very often life and work get in the way, and our busy lives limit the time we can spend in the kitchen. However, we are all also becoming increasingly aware of the important connections between following a healthy lifestyle and cooking our own food at home. With this in mind, I've included a diverse collection of accessible and practical recipes in this book so that, even on the busiest days, you can enjoy wholesome and satisfying meals at home.

Whether you choose to cook one of the quick-and-easy recipes or a slightly more elaborate one, exploring an unfamiliar cuisine can seem daunting. The good news is that Moroccan cooking is more accessible than you might imagine. It often calls for familiar ingredients and straightforward cooking methods, making it very approachable. In fact, the tools as well as the ingredients required to develop madaq may already be in your kitchen, waiting to be transformed into something magical and delicious. In this chapter, I share with you my trusted list of must-have ingredients and equipment.

INGREDIENTS

SPICES AND OTHER SEASONINGS

CUMIN: Cumin has a warm, earthy flavor with delicate hints of citrus. Both the seeds and the ground spice are used, adding a unique character to various spice blends and many traditional recipes.

CORIANDER: Coriander seeds, whole or ground, are another essential spice in Moroccan cuisine. Coriander is distinctively aromatic and has a citrusy, nutty flavor that enhances many dishes.

SWEET PAPRIKA: Sweet paprika is prized for its ability to add a vibrant color and a gentle warmth, with a touch of sweetness, to many dishes.

SMOKED SWEET PAPRIKA: Smoked sweet paprika isn't traditional in Moroccan cooking, but I like the unexpected twist it can bring to classic dishes. Mild and sweet, it contributes a subtle smokiness.

CINNAMON: Cinnamon is cherished for its remarkable ability to bring a sweet and warm flavor to many dishes, from its comforting embrace of baked goods to the delightful balance it provides in both sweet and savory preparations.

GINGER: Ground ginger adds a distinctive warmth and pungent notes to many tagines, enhancing and deepening their flavors.

TURMERIC: With its vibrant yellow color and slightly bitter, earthy flavor, turmeric is one of the stars of Moroccan cuisine. It is used in many tagines and traditional couscous recipes, where it also paints the dishes with a sunny hue.

SAFFRON: Aromatic, with a slightly floral and bitter flavor, saffron threads are used in many tagines, which they imbue with a distinctive yellow color.

CAYENNE PEPPER: Cayenne pepper, known for its fiery spiciness, is a potent player in the Moroccan kitchen. It is usually used in moderation, as its heat can be quite intense.

GREEN CARDAMOM: Sweet, aromatic green cardamom, is used in many baked goods, and it is one of the identifying flavors of Moroccan coffee.

ANISEED: Aniseed and ground anise are used to add a licorice-like flavor to a variety of baked goods and other sweet treats.

FENNEL SEEDS: Fennel contributes a flavor that's like a gentle embrace of anise with a delicate hint of sweetness.

RAS EL HANOUT: The origins of this ubiquitous spice blend can be traced back to ancient times, but its essence becomes clear when you translate its name: "ras el hanout" means "top of the shop" in Arabic, indicating that it is made with the finest spices in each merchant's store. There's no fixed recipe for this blend—instead, it reflects the artistry of the individual spice purveyor. (To make your own ras el hanout, see the recipe on page 38.)

BLACK PEPPER: The recipes in this book were tested with ordinary black pepper, but my favorite type is actually the long pepper, also known as Indian long pepper or Indian pepper, as it is native to that country. It has a distinctive fragrance and floral aroma, with a hint of ginger, that I find very special; you can order it online from specialty spice purveyors. To grind long pepper, you can use a coffee or spice grinder, or chop it into smaller pieces and use a standard pepper mill.

SALT

When I am cooking at home, my go-to choice is fine sea salt. I like it for its small grains, natural flavor, and high mineral content. Nevertheless, feel free to choose a different type of salt—but be sure to adjust the amount accordingly. For example, because of the larger crystal size, a teaspoon of kosher or coarse salt will not deliver the same amount of saltiness as a teaspoon of fine sea salt. As a general rule, when I am trying a new recipe, I usually add about half of the specified quantity of salt and then adjust to taste if necessary.

HERBS

PARSLEY: Parsley is used to enhance the flavors of many Moroccan dishes, from salads to tagines. It brings a burst of color and a hint of herbal freshness.

CILANTRO: Cilantro adds fresh, citrusy notes to countless Moroccan dishes, from hearty tagines and couscous to salads, marinades, and condiments. It is also known as fresh coriander, as the dried seeds of the same plant are the spice we know by that name.

Feel free to substitute parsley for cilantro, or vice versa, based on your preference.

MINT: Mint in some ways encapsulates the essence of Moroccan cuisine. It's a vital element of many dishes, bringing refreshing and aromatic notes. Whether it's used in a fragrant mint tea, as a garnish, or as an integral ingredient in a salad, it adds a welcome revitalizing note.

CONDIMENTS

HARISSA: Harissa is the queen of Moroccan condiments. It's a fiery red chile paste made from dried chiles. Whether used as a flavor base in marinades for grilled meats or mixed with mayonnaise to make a dipping sauce for French fries, harissa adds a fragrant heat and a complex depth of flavor to many dishes. In the United States, I particularly like the brand Mina. Their harissa pastes, red and green, have an authentic taste, and they are as delicious as the pastes you can purchase in Morocco. In the UK, where I live, my go-to brands are Amboora for when I want a fierce, punchy harissa and Belazu for a milder, smokier one. (To make your own red or green harissa, see the recipes on pages 44 and 47.)

GREEN HARISSA: Made with fresh chiles rather than dried, green harissa is the invigorating counterpart to red harissa. Bursting with fresh herbs, spices, and green chile peppers, it brings tangy heat to many dishes.

PRESERVED LEMONS: Preserved lemons are an essential part of Moroccan cuisine. Most commonly used in tagines and cooked salads, they have a distinctive subtly bitter, sharp flavor characterized by a light saltiness. Preserved lemons are now available in specialty shops and some supermarkets in the US, but the quality varies (some are extremely salty). (To make your own preserved lemons, see the recipe on page 41.) When working with preserved lemons, most Moroccans use only the rind, either chopped and stirred into a dish or thinly sliced for a garnish. However, I prefer to just seed them and then finely chop them whole, including both flesh and peel. A little bit goes a long way: I recommend adding half of the quantity specified in the recipe to start, then tasting and adding more, if desired.

COUSCOUS AND FLOUR

COUSCOUS: Couscous grains are made using a unique process: coarse-ground durum wheat flour is moistened with water and rolled into tiny pellets, which are then gently steamed to create small, beadlike grains. Couscous is a staple of Moroccan cuisine, and it is much more than just a side dish. In Morocco, the term "couscous" actually refers to a dish made of couscous topped with meat or chicken and vegetables in a fragrant broth. Traditionally, it is prepared in a special pot called a couscoussière, also known as a couscous steamer. It consists of two parts: a large bottom pot, where vegetables and meat are simmered in broth, and a perforated pot, or basket, that sits on top of it. The couscous grains are steamed in the perforated basket, absorbing the flavors of the broth as they cook and become light and fluffy. Outside Morocco, the most common method for preparing couscous is the instant one, where the couscous is put in a bowl, boiling water is poured over it, and the grains are covered and left to steam. However, the grains often end up overcooked and soggy. When using the instant method, it's important not to add too much water and to be careful not to let the couscous steam for too long. For either method, once the couscous is just cooked, adding a small amount of fat, such as a knob of butter or a little olive oil, and using a fork to fluff it up, will enhance its texture. For my trusted method for preparing fluffy couscous, see Fragrant Chicken and Onions Buried in Couscous—Seffa Medfouna (page 163).

FINE AND COARSE SEMOLINA FLOUR: Made from durum wheat, semolina flour, with a coarse texture and rich flavor, is the base of many traditional breads and pastries. Fine semolina flour is used for breads such as batbout (20-Minute Panfried Bread, page 86) and m'semen (Garlic Butter and Cheese Flatbreads, page 75), while dishes like harcha (Semolina Bread with Salted Honey Butter, page 60) and assida (Brown Butter Semolina Porridge, page 85) are made with coarse semolina flour.

LEGUMES

CHICKPEAS: Whether it's in classic dishes like couscous or harira, or in street foods like tayb o'hari ("Tayb O'hari" Chickpeas, Tuna, and Egg Salad, page 219), chickpeas are an essential ingredient in Moroccan cooking. Their nutty flavor and firm texture make them the perfect addition to a wide range of dishes. (Chickpeas are also called garbanzo beans.)

CANNELLINI BEANS: Cannellini beans, although not native to Morocco, have found a place in many recipes. The creamy, ivory beans add a mild, nutty flavor and texture to a variety of hearty dishes.

BROWN LENTILS: Brown lentils, also not native to Morocco, have become part of the Moroccan pantry, used in recipes like Harira (page 140), the hearty soup, and adis (Lentil Stew with Sun-Dried Tomatoes and Kale, page 135).

NUTS AND DRIED FRUITS

DATES: With their natural sweetness and rich, caramel flavor, dates are a favorite ingredient, enjoyed as a snack and used in sweet preparations like zaazaa (Avocado and Almond Smoothie, page 81). They are harvested in Errachidia and Ouarzazate, between October and November.

DRIED APRICOTS: Dried apricots, with their unique combination of tangy and sweet flavors, are traditionally used in tagines. I also love to include them in salads and desserts, where they offer a burst of sunshine in every bite.

PRUNES: Sweet, slightly tart prunes are used in a variety of tagines, where they add a touch of complexity.

ALMONDS: Almonds add texture, flavor, and a touch of richness to many dishes, both sweet and savory. They are the star of sweet pastries such as Almond Macaroons (page 268), and toasted almonds are used to garnish many tagines and salads.

PISTACHIOS: While not native to Morocco, pistachios have become part of the country's culinary repertoire. I use them to flavor a range of dishes, from tagines to salads to desserts, and as a garnish.

WALNUTS AND PECANS: Both pecans and walnuts are enjoyed as a wholesome snack; in baking and cooking, they are often used interchangeably, although pecans are milder and sweeter than walnuts. Both nuts are commonly added to stuffings and salads, among other dishes.

OILS AND OTHER FATS

OLIVE OIL: For me, olive oil is not just a cooking medium but also a symbol of the Mediterranean essence deeply ingrained in Moroccan cooking traditions. I generally prefer extra-virgin olive oil because of its flavor and higher nutritional value than ordinary olive oil. However, for the recipes in this book, you can use the type that best suits your taste and budget. Although they are more expensive, I do recommend cold-pressed oils (also referred to as "cold-extracted") for dressings and for drizzling over finished dishes. Cold-pressed olive oil is processed using only mechanical means, without heat or chemicals, preserving its flavor and more of its nutrients.

ARGAN OIL: Argan oil, with a distinctive nutty flavor and rich, amber hue, is sometimes referred to as "liquid gold" in Morocco. To Moroccans, argan oil is more than just a cooking staple—it's a vital part of our lifestyle and our culinary tradition, and it offers impressive health benefits, including anti-inflammatory properties; it is also high in unsaturated fats. However, argan oil can be quite pricey outside of Morocco; walnut oil, with a comparable nutty flavor, is a decent, more budget-friendly substitute.

GHEE: Ghee, Indian clarified butter, isn't commonly used in Moroccan cooking, but I find it to be the best substitute for s'men, which is nearly impossible to source outside Morocco. S'men is clarified fermented butter that is often used in preparations such as Tangia Marrakchia (see Cumin and Preserved-Lemon Beef Stew, page 198) or to enhance the texture and flavor of couscous grains.

FLORAL WATERS

ROSE WATER: Rose water, with its delicate floral aroma, is usually showcased in sweet pastries and desserts. A few drops of rose water can transform a simple treat into an aromatic delight.

ORANGE BLOSSOM WATER: Orange blossom water, with its citrusy aroma and flavor, also plays a significant role in pastries and both sweet and savory dishes.

The quality of the floral water you use can have a considerable impact on your recipe. I recommend purchasing waters that are made with minimal ingredients (check the label: preferably just distilled water and natural orange blossom or rose extract). Avoid products with synthetic additives or preservatives. If you have the opportunity to smell or taste the water before purchasing it, do so. It should have a pleasant, floral aroma and a delicate flavor.

OTHER INGREDIENTS

GUNPOWDER GREEN TEA: Gunpowder green tea is a Chinese green tea variety known for its tightly rolled leaves that resemble small pellets of gunpowder. The leaves are hand-rolled during processing, which helps preserve their flavor and aroma. Introduced to Morocco through European trade routes in the nineteenth century, this tea quickly became an essential part of Moroccan tea culture. Its slightly smoky, robust taste makes it the ideal base for traditional Moroccan mint tea.

OLIVES: We're lucky to enjoy a wide variety of olives in Morocco, ranging in color from various shades of green to deep purple and black. With their distinctive briny, tangy taste, they add depth to tagines and bring vibrancy to salads and many other dishes. Cured or dried black olives (used in the Orange and Black-Olive Radicchio Salad; page 98), with an intense flavor and wrinkled appearance, can be difficult to find outside of Morocco. If you're unable to source them online, use regular black or purple brined olives such as California black olives or Kalamata.

STOCKS: I call for beef, chicken, and vegetable stocks in the recipes in this book. For recipe testing, I used low-sodium stock, and I recommend that you do the same; if your stock is salted, add less salt than called for in the recipe and then adjust the seasoning to your taste.

RED AND WHITE VINEGARS: Invest in good-quality vinegars for your dressings: they will have a real impact on the final result. Avoid those labeled "distilled vinegar," which are usually made from industrial alcohols and lack depth and flavor.

ALMOND BUTTER: Almond butter, preferably made from roasted almonds, is one of the main ingredients of Amlou, a paste made from honey, argan oil, and almond butter (page 49). Make sure you source a natural one with no added sugars, oils, salt, or preservatives. It may separate as it stands; just stir it before use.

GRATED TOMATOES: Morocco has juicy, flavorful tomatoes almost year-round which are often used grated in soups, tagines, and many other dishes. When fresh tomatoes aren't available, canned ones are often used instead. As a general rule, I substitute four grated fresh tomatoes for one 14.5-ounce can of diced tomatoes. See page 20 for a tip on grating tomatoes using a box grater.

KITCHEN EQUIPMENT

TAGINE POTS VS. MODERN COOKWARE

You don't necessarily need a clay tagine pot. That's a strong statement and probably one you wouldn't expect in a Moroccan cookbook, considering that a tagine is the most emblematic Moroccan dish there is, but let me explain. The word "tagine" refers to both the traditional earthenware pot used for cooking a tagine and the dish itself. Historically, the nomads of North Africa used tagines as portable ovens, enabling them to prepare meals when they were on the move. A traditional tagine pot is made of clay. The round base is wide and shallow, and its conical lid sits tightly on it; together, they constitute a sort of earthenware oven. The pot is placed over a very low flame for cooking and as the food cooks slowly, steam rises into the conical top, resulting in condensation, and then that liquid falls back down into the dish, essentially constantly basting the ingredients and keeping them moist and tender. The cooking process involved is actually very similar to that used for stews and braises.

Preparing a tagine the traditional way in a clay pot can be a special experience, deeply rooted in Moroccan culture. However, these pots demand a significant amount of time and care. They require proper seasoning and careful maintenance to prevent cracks or other damage, and their fragility makes breakage a concern. As a result, the majority of Moroccans today are more likely to opt for the convenience and sturdiness of metal pots or pressure cookers. For the same reasons, the tagine recipes in this cookbook were all tested in ordinary pots or large deep cast-iron or other heavy-bottomed frying pans. My intention here wasn't to discourage you from making a tagine in a traditional clay pot but rather to let you know that it's perfectly fine if you don't. Depending on the type of tagine, my tagine recipes variously call for a large pot, a Dutch oven, or a large frying pan.

I do enjoy cooking in a traditional tagine pot, especially when I have the time to slow down and appreciate the process; I own a few tagine clay pots that I have brought back with me from Morocco over the years. If you'd like to buy a tagine pot, the abundance of options on the market might make purchasing the right one seem daunting. Along with traditional clay pots, you can find tagine-shaped pots crafted from cast iron or aluminum, but in my opinion, a traditional clay pot remains the best choice. The unique properties of clay, aka terra-cotta, when the dish is heated gradually, create a humid environment that lets the food simmer beautifully and allows for the full release of all the flavors of the ingredients, for a truly authentic taste. Clay pots also introduce a very subtle earthy or mineral note to the foods cooked in them, adding a touch of complexity and depth. But if you opt for a clay pot, you will need to adjust the cooking times in these recipes. Because clay tagine pots can tolerate only relatively low temperatures, the time needed for each step will be noticeably longer than the timings given in those recipes.

FOOD PROCESSOR

I'm not fond of cluttering my kitchen with gadgets, but a food processor is really an absolute must-have. It's a versatile appliance that simplifies countless food preparation tasks and will save you a lot of time. I use mine regularly to chop herbs or nuts, to make sauces and marinades.

BOX GRATER

Along with its typical uses, such as shredding cheese or potatoes or other vegetables, a box grater is commonly used in Morocco to grate tomatoes to be used in sauces and tagines. To do so, first cut the tomatoes crosswise in half. Then, with a firm grip, press the cut side of one half against the large holes of the grater and carefully grate the tomato until only the skin remains in your hand. Repeat the technique with the other tomato halves. Be sure to reserve all the juices.

GARLIC PRESS

This is one of my most used kitchen tools. A simple squeeze effortlessly transforms whole garlic cloves into perfectly minced bits, saving me precious time and effort.

MICRO GRATER

I first used a micro grater at cooking school, and it quickly became an indispensable tool. Although initially I used it just for grating lemon zest, I quickly realized that its remarkable versatility extended to grating garlic cloves as well as nutmeg or fresh ginger.

KITCHEN SCALE

I know that in the United States, it's common practice to measure many ingredients with cup measures. Because of that, I have included volume (cup) measures whenever appropriate for ingredients in this book. However, for those, like myself, who prefer the precision of a scale, I have also included the weights of any ingredients above 15 grams. I strongly encourage you to use a kitchen scale. Although it might seem like more effort at first, once you're accustomed to using a scale, it becomes an intuitive and efficient habit that will actually simplify the cooking process. And its precision will give you more consistent results, especially in baking, where accurate measurements can greatly influence the outcome of a recipe.

COOKING TIPS

Our personal relationships with cooking are as diverse as the flavors of a generously spiced tagine. Some of us revel in the kitchen and wish we had more time to cook, while others genuinely do not enjoy the cooking process. Nevertheless, for many of us, cooking for ourselves and our families is a necessity.

Regardless of your level of expertise in the kitchen, the list of tips below should help make your kitchen experience more efficient—and more enjoyable.

IN THE KITCHEN

Invest in good-quality equipment. Good-quality kitchen equipment, such as sharp knives and durable pots and pans, can make cooking more enjoyable and efficient. That said, don't feel pressured to purchase a lot of new equipment at once. Take your time to build your collection progressively. My first kitchen investment was a special chef's knife.

BE ORGANIZED. The mise-en-place principle is the art of preparation. Before you begin cooking, take the time to gather all the necessary ingredients and utensils. Chop, slice, and measure everything you'll need and arrange it neatly within arm's reach. This practice not only streamlines the cooking process but also instills a sense of order in the kitchen. It reduces stress and helps prevent errors.

KEEP A TRASH BOWL HANDY. This is a simple tip, but it can save a lot of time. I always have a bowl on the counter to collect food scraps and trash as I cook. It's an easy way to keep your workspace tidy.

CLEAN UP AS YOU GO. Cooking is more enjoyable in an uncluttered kitchen. Clean up as you go by washing utensils and cutting boards while the food cooks. This reduces post-cooking cleanup and keeps your workspace organized as well.

KEEP IT SIMPLE. Don't feel pressured to create elaborate dishes: simple meals can be just as delicious and satisfying. Begin with straightforward recipes that have minimal ingredients and steps. Then, as you gain confidence and experience, you can move on to more complex dishes.

THINK OF RECIPES AS GUIDES. Before you start cooking, carefully read through the entire recipe. This will give you a clear understanding of the overall process and let you avoid surprises along the way. Pay attention to the order of ingredients, cooking times, and techniques. But after you've prepared a recipe once as written and are feeling confident about the result, you can experiment with adjustments and substitutions as you like.

USE ALL YOUR SENSES. Engage your sense of sight, smell, and even sound when you cook. Listen for sizzling, observe color changes, and inhale the aromas to judge the progress of your dish. Using your senses will also help you develop an intuitive understanding of the flavor profiles and doneness of the food you are cooking.

TASTE AS YOU GO. Tasting as you cook is not just about adjusting seasoning; it's about connecting with the process and understanding how flavors develop. As you gain experience, experiment with balancing flavors. Achieving a well-balanced dish often involves considering the five basic tastes: sweet, salty, sour, bitter, and umami. Often a dish you are unhappy with can be saved by simply adjusting one of these elements. It's a skill that comes with experience and time, but never underestimate the power of a simple squeeze of lemon or a drizzle of honey to balance out acidity or sweetness.

LABEL AND DATE EVERYTHING. When packing dishes you've prepared into containers (or heavy-duty plastic bags) for storing in the fridge or freezer, label and date them. This way, you can easily keep track of what you have on hand and ensure that you use these items while they are still at their best.

USE LEFTOVERS CREATIVELY. Reinvent leftovers for new meals. For example, turn yesterday's grilled chicken into tacos, or incorporate those roasted vegetables into a hearty grain bowl.

AT THE MARKET

Cooking starts with your shopping cart. Take a moment to evaluate each item you choose. For fruits and vegetables, look for vibrant colors, smooth unblemished skin, and signs of ripeness. Similarly, make it a habit to read labels and the ingredients lists of ready-made products such as condiments and stocks, being mindful about additives or preservatives.

SEEK OUT SEASONAL INGREDIENTS. Produce that is in season is often cheaper; buying it supports local agriculture; and, most important, it offers you peak flavor. Embrace the abundance of each season by experimenting with different fruits and vegetables at their peak.

BEING ORGANIZED

KEEP A WELL-STOCKED PANTRY. Having a pantry stocked with staples such as couscous, rice, pasta, canned tomatoes, spices, and olive oil ensures that you always have the basics of a quick and easy meal on hand. When I am not in the mood to prepare dinner, knowing I have a full pantry encourages me to make the most of it.

MAKE SURE YOUR SPICES ARE FRESH. The quality and freshness of your spices, particularly ground ones, play an important role in the taste of your dishes. Buy spices from a reliable source, and don't forget to check expiration dates. To check their freshness, look for bright colors and an appealing fragrance, whether you are smelling them directly from the jar or rubbing the spice between your fingers.

MEAL PLANNING. If you can, plan your meals for the upcoming week, or even just for the next few days. This will help you organize your shopping list and also save time, since you won't have to think about what you will be cooking every single night.

BATCH COOKING. I wouldn't consider myself someone who preps every meal in advance as much as possible at the start of each week, but I do practice batch cooking. Every Saturday or Sunday, I prepare a large batch of at least one recipe, often a tagine, that can be enjoyed over several days. Additionally, I make sure there's a ready-to-go cooked carb, like couscous, or some roasted vegetables in the fridge. Then it's easy to pair these with a quickly cooked protein or add to a big salad. This can be a great time-saver on busy days.

AND, FINALLY . . .

Be kind to yourself, and don't fear mistakes. When a dish doesn't turn out as planned, view it as an opportunity to understand what went wrong and how to improve it next time. Every great cook has experienced failures, and it's these experiences that have helped refine their skills. The more you cook, the more comfortable you'll become in the kitchen. Over time, you'll build confidence and discover your own culinary strengths as well as likes and dislikes.

CELEBRATE YOUR ACHIEVEMENTS. Preparing a delicious meal, whether just for yourself or for others, is a rewarding experience. Acknowledge your achievements, no matter how modest, and use them as stepping-stones to greater culinary experiments. Confidence in the kitchen is not just about skills—it's also about recognizing and appreciating your own journey.

COOK WITH OTHERS WHENEVER YOU CAN! Cooking with friends or family can be both fun and educational. You can exchange tips and ideas and learn from one another while creating memories.

HOW TO CHOOSE THE PERFECT RECIPE

My hope is for *Madaq* to become a book that always has a place in your kitchen, a trusted companion that helps you create delicious meals in a stress-free way. The main question that guided me while developing the recipes was how to make each one so that the result would be with little effort and lots of madaq. This meant prioritizing time and efficiency, along with keeping the utensils and cookware needed to a minimum. With that in mind, I've put together recipe lists that will allow you to find them according to preparation time, cook time, and/or occasion. This way, you can easily choose the perfect recipe according to your own needs.

Weekday Dinners: ready in 35 minutes or less

Effortless Meals: ready in 60 minutes or less

Baked Chermoula Potatoes with Eggs–Batata M'chermla (page 59)

Beans on Toast with Harissa Oil–Loubia (page 82)

Peach and Tomato Salad with Orange Blossom and Honey Dressing (page 97)

Charred Cabbage with Harissa and Peanut Butter Sauce (page 121)

Zaalouk and Gruyère Grilled Cheese Sandwiches (page 132)

Lentil Stew with Sun-Dried Tomatoes and Kale–Adis (page 135)

Ras el Hanout Mushroom Tacos with Tomato and Cucumber Salad (page 122)

Egg and Tomato Tagine with Tangy Cilantro Oil (page 144)

Sticky Orange and Turmeric Chicken Skewers (page 156)

Sheet-Pan Chicken with Spiced Grapes, Chickpeas, and Thyme (page 167)

Sheet-Pan Chicken with Potatoes, Preserved Lemon, and Olives (page 168)

Chicken Berkoukes Soup (page 172)

Beef Skewers with Dill and Lemon Chermoula (page 187)

Kefta and Kale Couscous Bowls (page 188)

Likama Smash Cheeseburgers with Smoky Harissa Sauce (page 197)

"Tayb O'hari" Chickpeas, Tuna, and Egg Salad (page 219)

Chermoula Salmon with Quick-Pickled Cucumbers (page 223)

Jalapeño Shrimp Tagine "Pil Pil" (page 231)

Seafood Berkoukes (page 234)

Easy Appetizers and Sides: 15 minutes prep time or less

Cumin and Parsley Potato Salad (page 94)

Harissa Caesar Salad with Crispy Spiced Chickpeas (page 101)

Peach and Tomato Salad with Orange Blossom and Honey Dressing (page 97)

Orange and Black-Olive Radicchio Salad (page 98)

Green Beans in Garlicky Oil–"Bil Zeit" (page 105)

Eggplant Dip with Red Bell Pepper–Zaalouk (page 106)

Triple-Lemon Charred Broccolini with Breadcrumbs (page 109)

Zucchini with Parsley and Garlicky Warm Croutons (page 113)

Roasted Moroccan Olives with Feta (page 110)

Spiced Carrots with Almonds, Olives, and Herbs (page 102)

Tagines and Soups: one-pot wonders

Batch Cooking: to enjoy throughout the week

Kid-Friendly: meals even picky eaters will love

Baked Chermoula Potatoes with Eggs–Batata M'chermla (page 59)

Beans on Toast with Harissa Oil–Loubia (page 82)

Eggplant Dip with Red Bell Pepper–Zaalouk (page 106)

Triple-Lemon Charred Broccolini with Breadcrumbs (page 109)

Lentil Stew with Sun-Dried Tomatoes and Kale–Adis (page 135)

Oven-Baked Cornflake-Crusted Chicken Tenders with Sweet Chermoula Sauce (page 159)

Quick Chicken Bastilla Puff Pies (page 153)

Sheet-Pan Chicken with Potatoes, Preserved Lemon, and Olives (page 168)

Chicken Berkoukes Soup (page 172)

Chermoula Salmon with Quick-Pickled Cucumbers (page 223)

Fish "Meatballs" and Tomato Tagine (page 227)

Seafood Berkoukes (page 234)

Weekend Projects: when you have time to slow down

Honey-Buttered Pancakes with Orange Blossom and Blueberry Sauce–Baghrir (page 69)

Garlic Butter and Cheese Flatbreads–M'semen (page 75)

Sesame and Aniseed Brioche–Krachel (page 63)

"Bakoula" Greens Galette with Burrata (page 125)

Fried Potato Cakes with Green Pepper and Tomato Salsa–Maakouda (page 67)

Chicken and Lentils in Onion Sauce with Pasta–Pappardelle R'fissa (page 150)

Chicken Tagine à l'Orange (page 160)

Fragrant Chicken and Onions Buried in Couscous–Seffa Medfouna (page 163)

Berber Stuffed Flatbreads–Aghroum Boutgouri (page 191)

Beef Short Ribs with Prunes (page 193)

Preserved Beef–Express Khlii (page 73)

Cumin and Preserved-Lemon Beef Stew–Tangia Marrekchia (page 198)

Lamb Covered in Tomatoes and Onions–Tagine Maqfoul (page 202)

Hasselback Butternut Squash with Merguez and Walnut (page 205)

Ras el Hanout Lamb Shoulder Méchoui with Pistachio and Apricot Salsa (page 210)

Pistachio Jawhara Cups (page 243)

Moroccan Mint Tea Chocolate Cheesecake (page 245)

Hands-Off Meals: 20 minutes prep time or less

Artichoke and Pea Tagine Pasta (page 139)

Lentil Stew with Sun-Dried Tomatoes and Kale–Adis (page 135)

Berber Vegetarian Skillet Tagine with Olive, Preserved Lemon, and Cilantro Salsa (page 136)

Creamy Preserved-Lemon Tomato Soup (page 143)

Egg and Tomato Tagine with Tangy Cilantro Oil (page 144)

Sheet-Pan Chicken with Potatoes, Preserved Lemon, and Olives (page 168)

Sheet-Pan Chicken with Spiced Grapes, Chickpeas, and Thyme (page 167)

Stuffed Chicken with Vermicelli and Chicken Liver–Djaj Maamer (page 171)

Cumin and Preserved-Lemon Beef Stew–Tangia Marrekchia (page 198)

Saffron Beef Chorba with Crispy Potatoes (page 181)

Kefta and Kale Couscous Bowls (page 188)

Ras el Hanout Lamb Shoulder Méchoui with Pistachio and Apricot Salsa (page 210)

Shrimp M'hammer Tagine (page 220)

Seafood Berkoukes (page 234)

Almond and Herb-Crusted Cod with T'faya (page 233)

Jalapeño Shrimp Tagine "Pil Pil" (page 231)

Chermoula Salmon with Quick-Pickled Cucumbers (page 223)

Quick-and-Easy Delights: sweet treats for anytime

Molten Chocolate Olive Oil Cake (page 249)

Brown Sugar, Apple, and Orange Blossom Cobbler with Brown Butter Topping (page 250)

Lemon and Almond Meskouta (page 255)

Ras el Hanout Chocolate Chip Banana Bread (page 258)

Spiced Affogato (page 261)

Amlou Cinnamon Knots (page 262)

Amlou Croissant Bread Pudding (page 78)

توابل

MADAQ FLAVOR BOOSTERS

SPICE BLENDS, CONDIMENTS, AND MORE TO USE EVERY DAY

This chapter contains recipes for my "flavor boosters" that I return to over and over again. I find that having these flavor boosters prepped and ready in my kitchen is a big game-changer. They help reduce the stress of meal preparation and allow me to effortlessly add a burst of deliciousness to any dish. With them on hand, you can quickly stir-fry pieces of chicken in the spice blend likama, prepare a simple salad with Orange Blossom and Honey Dressing (page 48), spread some amlou on your morning toast, or just stir a teaspoon of green harissa into eggs for an omelette—the options are endless. From the vibrant warmth of ras el hanout to the scented kick of preserved lemons, these flavor boosters are the key to both effortless weeknight suppers and dinner party dishes that are infused with bold Moroccan flavors.

likama spice blend

"Likama" translates as "spices" in Moroccan Arabic, and this blend is made with seven of the spices most commonly used in Moroccan cooking. It doesn't have as many spices as Ras el Hanout (page 38), making it more versatile. Likama is traditionally used to season tagines, roasts, or grilled meats and poultry, but I like to add it to marinades for roasted vegetables such as potatoes or zucchini.

makes 1¼ cups (50 g)

- 1 tablespoon ground ginger
- 1 tablespoon ground turmeric
- 1 tablespoon sweet paprika
- 1 tablespoon ground cumin
- 1 tablespoon ground coriander
- 1½ teaspoons white pepper
- A dozen gratings of fresh nutmeg

1 Combine the ginger, turmeric, paprika, cumin, coriander, white pepper, and nutmeg in a small container and mix well. Seal the container and store in a cool, dark place, such as your kitchen cupboard.

ras el hanout

makes 1⁄3 cup (50 g)

"Ras el hanout," literally meaning "top of the shop" in Arabic, refers to the tradition of making this spice blend, a Moroccan staple, with the finest ingredients in the merchant's shop. Known for its perfumed scent, earthy tones, and subtle sweetness, it's often used to season meat dishes such as lamb shoulder (page 210). It's one of my favorite spice blends, and I incorporate it into a variety of vegetarian dishes, such as my mushroom tacos (page 122). This version calls for preground spices for the sake of convenience, but if you have time, I encourage you to use whole spices and grind them with a coffee grinder or mortar and pestle. The result will be fresher and far more robust.

- 1 tablespoon ground turmeric
- 1 tablespoon ground ginger
- 1 tablespoon sweet paprika
- 1 tablespoon ground cumin
- 1 tablespoon ground coriander
- 2 teaspoons ground allspice
- 1 teaspoon ground cinnamon
- 1 teaspoon ground cardamom
- 10 gratings of fresh nutmeg or 1⁄2 teaspoon ground nutmeg
- 1⁄2 teaspoon ground cloves
- 1⁄2 teaspoon black pepper
- 1 tablespoon dried rose petals (optional)

1 Combine the turmeric, ginger, paprika, cumin, coriander, allspice, cinnamon, cardamom, nutmeg, cloves, pepper, and rose petals, if using, in a small container and stir to mix. Seal the container and store in a cool, dark place, such as a kitchen cupboard.

classic chermoula

makes 3⁄4 cup (150 g)

Chermoula is a cornerstone of Moroccan cuisine and the backbone of countless dishes. It is most often used as a marinade, but it can also be served as a condiment. It is typically made with cilantro, parsley, spices, lemon juice, and olive oil, but every region or family has its own version. Warm spices such as cumin and sweet paprika add depth of flavor, and other ingredients such as saffron, tomato paste, or preserved lemons may also be included. I usually keep my basic chermoula simple, making it more versatile, but see the following pages for two of my favorite variations. Traditionally chermoula is prepared in a mortar and pestle, but you can chop the herbs by hand or in a food processor. When it is used as a marinade, chermoula infuses fish or chicken or other proteins with flavor and also tenderizes them slightly because of the acidity of the lemon juice. Served as a condiment, it adds a burst of fresh flavor to dishes such as grilled meats, pasta, or rice.

Chermoula is best when freshly made, but it can be stored in a sealed container in the fridge for up to 3 days; its flavor will mellow slightly over time.

- 5 tablespoons (75 g) olive oil
- 3 garlic cloves, minced or pressed
- 1 cup (18 g) cilantro leaves and tender stems, finely chopped
- 1 cup (18 g) flat-leaf parsley leaves and tender stems, finely chopped
- 2 tablespoons (30 g) fresh lemon juice
- 2 teaspoons sweet paprika
- 2 teaspoons ground cumin
- 1 teaspoon fine sea salt
- Generous pinch of granulated sugar

1 Combine the olive oil, garlic, cilantro, parsley, lemon juice, paprika, cumin, salt, and sugar in a medium bowl and mix well. The chermoula can be kept in a sealed container in the fridge for up to 3 days.

preserved lemons

makes 6 preserved lemons

Preserved lemons, a staple ingredient in Moroccan cuisine, add a unique flavor to tagines such as Eggplant Tagine M'qualli (page 129) and cooked salads such as bakoula ("Bakoula" Greens Galette with Burrata, page 125). They impart a fragrant, citrusy punch that goes beyond simple tartness and elevates the entire dish. Preserved lemons are simple to make—the key ingredient is time. It takes about a month to preserve the lemons, but the longer they age, the more fragrant and softer they become; kept refrigerated, they can be stored for up to a year. In fact, preserved lemons that are months old are often the most flavorful ones. Sometimes a lacy white coating will appear on the fruit, but this doesn't mean that their shelf life has expired; just rinse it off and use them as you normally would. For the best results, I recommend using unwaxed organic lemons with a dark-yellow color (indicating they are riper than paler fruits) and thin skin. These will allow the salt to penetrate them more thoroughly, resulting in more flavorful lemons.

- 6 lemons (480 g), ideally unwaxed and organic
- ¼ cup (70 g) fine sea salt
- ¾ to 1⅓ cups (170 to 255 g) fresh lemon juice (from about 4 to 6 large lemons), or as needed

1 Choose a glass jar with a tight-fitting lid large enough to hold the tightly compressed prepared lemons; if necessary, use two jars. Wash the lemons thoroughly and pat them dry with a clean cloth. Cut a deep slit lengthwise down the center of each lemon, stopping about 1 inch (2.5 cm) from the stem end. Make another cut perpendicular to the first one to form a cross, stopping 1 inch (2.5 cm) from the end again. (You will end up with lemons cut into quarters that are still attached at the stem end.) Fill the cuts in each lemon with about 2 teaspoons salt, then reshape them back into whole lemons.

2 Pack the lemons into the jar(s) and pour in the lemon juice. It's important that the lemons be pressed down in the jar(s) and packed as tightly as possible to allow them to release their juices during the preservation process.

3 Set the jar in a cool, dark place, such as your kitchen cupboard, and let stand for about 4 weeks, giving the jar(s) a good shake once a week to evenly redistribute the salt and lemon juice. After 1 month, transfer the jar(s) to the fridge; refrigerated, the preserved lemons will keep for up to 1 year.

dill and lemon chermoula

makes ¾ cup (180 g)

This variation of classic Chermoula (page 38) retains the marinade's distinctive flavor notes while introducing a bolder lemon taste along with an untraditional and, in my opinion, underrated herb: dill. Use it as a sauce for rice or pasta, as well as a marinade for any meat or chicken or vegetables. The recipe calls for finely chopped herbs, but you can simply toss all the ingredients into a food processor and let it do the work for you.

- 5 tablespoons (75 g) olive oil
- 3 garlic cloves, minced or pressed
- Zest of 2 lemons (15 g), removed in strips with a vegetable peeler and minced
- ½ cup (9 g) cilantro leaves and tender stems, finely chopped
- ½ cup (9 g) flat-leaf parsley leaves and tender stems, finely chopped
- ¼ cup (24 g) dill sprigs, finely chopped
- 2 tablespoons (30 g) fresh lemon juice
- 2 teaspoons sweet paprika
- 2 teaspoons ground cumin
- 1 teaspoon fine sea salt
- Generous pinch of granulated sugar

1 Combine the olive oil, garlic, lemon zest, cilantro, parsley, dill, lemon juice, paprika, cumin, salt, and sugar in a medium bowl and stir to mix. Or combine all the ingredients in a food processor and pulse to mix. The chermoula can be kept in a sealed container in the fridge for up to 3 days.

sweet chermoula

makes ¾ cup (235 g)

This variation on classic Chermoula (page 38) adds a touch of sweetness with honey and a hint of smokiness with smoked paprika. It's a versatile marinade, suitable for grilling or roasting a variety of proteins as well as vegetables, and ideal for those moments when I want a change from the traditional version but still crave Moroccan flavors. It also makes a flavorful spread for sandwiches or an unusual dipping sauce for fries and for dishes like my Cornflake-Crusted Chicken Tenders (page 159).

- 2 cups (36 g) cilantro leaves and tender stems, finely chopped
- ¼ cup (60 g) olive oil
- 3 tablespoons (66 g) honey
- 3 garlic cloves, minced or pressed
- 3 tablespoons (45 g) fresh lemon juice
- 1 tablespoon smoked sweet paprika (or substitute regular sweet paprika)
- 2 teaspoons ground cumin
- 1¼ teaspoons fine sea salt, or more to taste

1 Combine the cilantro, olive oil, honey, garlic, lemon juice, paprika, cumin, and salt in a medium bowl and mix well. Taste and adjust the seasoning, adding more salt if necessary. The chermoula can be kept in a sealed container in the fridge for up to 3 days.

orange and turmeric marinade

makes about ¾ cup (185 g)

This marinade is an easy way to add a touch of sunshine and spice to your weeknight meals. The orange juice tenderizes the proteins slightly and adds a hint of sweetness, while the turmeric brings warm, earthy notes and a beautiful golden color. For the most flavor, marinate your choice of ingredient for at least 2 hours, or as long as overnight. I often use this for chicken breasts or thighs, but for a lighter protein option, try it with salmon or halibut or another firm-fleshed fish. Or use it for vegetables like zucchini or eggplant before grilling them; they will soak up the marinade beautifully.

- 5 tablespoons (75 g) olive oil
- 3 garlic cloves, minced or pressed
- Grated zest of 2 oranges (about 2 packed teaspoons)
- ¼ cup (60 g) fresh orange juice
- 1 tablespoon honey
- 1 tablespoon dried mint
- 1½ teaspoons ground turmeric
- ¾ teaspoon fine sea salt, or more to taste

1 Combine the olive oil, garlic, orange zest, orange juice, honey, mint, turmeric, and salt in a small bowl and stir to mix. The marinade can be stored in a sealed container in the fridge for up to 3 days.

harissa

makes 1 cup (280 g)

Harissa is widely considered the queen of North African condiments. Its name comes from the Arabic word "harassa," which means "smash" or "pound," referring to the texture of the spicy chile paste when it is ground in a mehraz, the ancient version of a mortar and pestle. In Morocco, there are many types of harissa; some are prepared with fresh red chiles, others are based on dried chiles. I have a slight preference for the dried-chile version, with its distinctive smoky flavor. To me, harissa is magical because it is so versatile. I use it to add a kick to my morning eggs, mix it with mayonnaise for fries and sandwiches, and toss a teaspoon or so into marinades; it is one of my favorite "flavor boosters." If you prefer a milder harissa, reduce the number of chiles de árbol or omit them entirely.

- 9 large guajillo chiles (70 g) or other mild to medium-hot dried hot chiles, such as New Mexico or pasilla, or a combination
- 5 chiles de árbol, or to taste (see headnote)
- 1 tablespoon cumin seeds
- 1 tablespoon coriander seeds
- 1 tablespoon fennel seeds
- ¼ cup (60 g) olive oil, plus more to cover the harissa for storing
- 4 garlic cloves, minced or pressed
- 2 tablespoons (30 g) fresh lemon juice
- 2 teaspoons sweet paprika
- 2 teaspoons granulated sugar
- 1 teaspoon fine sea salt, or more to taste

1 Use scissors to cut the stems from the chiles, then slit them open from the top and scrape out the seeds. Put the chiles in a medium heatproof bowl and add enough boiling water to submerge the chiles. Cover with plastic wrap and let stand for 20 to 25 minutes, until the chiles are rehydrated, pliable, and cool enough to handle; drain. Be careful not to handle the softened chiles with your hands; use tongs or wear gloves.

2 Toast the cumin, coriander, and fennel seeds in a small dry frying pan over medium-low heat, stirring constantly with a wooden spatula or spoon, just until fragrant, about 1 to 2 minutes. (Overtoasting the seeds will give the harissa a bitter flavor.)

3 Transfer the seeds to a food processor or blender, add the olive oil, garlic, lemon juice, paprika, sugar, and salt, and process until the spices are ground and the mixture is smooth. Add the chiles and process until a coarse paste forms. Taste and adjust the seasoning, adding more salt, if desired. (If the harissa is very spicy, you may want to spread it on a bit of bread to taste it.)

4 Transfer the harissa to a jar and pour enough olive oil over the top of it to cover. Seal the jar and store in the fridge for up to 1 month.

harissa chile crisp

makes 1 cup (210 g)

Although I love all sorts of cuisines, I have a soft spot for the bold flavors of Chinese cooking, particularly its use of spicy Sichuan peppercorns and its never-ending range of fragrant, umami-packed condiments. I always have a jar of chile crisp in my fridge: it effortlessly adds a burst of heat and a delicious crunch to any dish it's drizzled on. Instead of the traditional Chinese version, try my Moroccan interpretation made with the warm, earthy spices of classic red harissa.

- 1 tablespoon cumin seeds
- 1 tablespoon fennel seeds
- 1 tablespoon coriander seeds
- 2 tablespoons sweet red pepper flakes, such as bell, Aleppo, or Urfa
- 2 teaspoons sweet paprika
- 2 teaspoons granulated garlic
- 2 teaspoons granulated onion
- 1 teaspoon granulated sugar
- ½ teaspoon hot red pepper flakes, or more to taste
- ¼ teaspoon fine sea salt, or more to taste
- ⅔ cup (160 g) olive oil

1 Toast the cumin, fennel, and coriander seeds in a small heavy frying pan over medium heat until fragrant, about 2 to 3 minutes. Transfer the toasted seeds to a mortar or coffee grinder and grind with the pestle or process until coarsely ground. Wipe out the pan and set aside.

2 Combine the ground toasted seeds, sweet red pepper flakes, paprika, granulated garlic and onion, sugar, hot red pepper flakes, and salt in a medium heatproof bowl.

3 Heat the olive oil in the pan you used to toast the spices over medium heat until it reaches 320°F (160°C); the oil should start to shimmer and small bubbles should form around a wooden spoon or chopstick if it is dipped into the oil. Carefully pour the hot oil over the spice mixture; let cool.

4 Transfer the chile crisp to an airtight glass jar and store in the fridge for up to 30 days. Bring to room temperature and stir before using.

green harissa

makes 1 cup (260 g)

Green harissa, cousin of the iconic red Harissa (page 44), is made with fresh green chiles rather than dried. It has a bright, herbaceous flavor with a pleasant touch of heat. Use it as you'd use any chile sauce or paste: add it to sandwiches or marinades, drizzle it over pasta, or stir into a stew; the possibilities are endless. While I love the smoky depth of the classic red harissa made with dried chiles, I particularly appreciate how this vibrant green version comes together in no time. Simply place all the ingredients in a food processor and process briefly—your green harissa is ready! I always keep a batch in my fridge for an easy flavor boost throughout the week.

- 7 jalapeños (6 ounces/170 g) or other fairly mild green chiles, stems removed and roughly sliced, seeds left in
- 1 cup (18 g) cilantro leaves and tender stems, roughly chopped
- 1 cup (18 g) flat-leaf parsley leaves and tender stems, roughly chopped
- 4 garlic cloves, roughly chopped
- 2½ teaspoons ground cumin
- ½ teaspoon fine sea salt, or more to taste
- ¼ teaspoon black pepper
- Large pinch of granulated sugar
- ¼ cup (60 g) olive oil

1 Combine the jalapeños, cilantro, parsley, garlic, cumin, salt, pepper, sugar, and olive oil in a food processor and process until a coarse paste forms. Taste and adjust the seasoning, adding more salt if necessary. Transfer to a sealed container and store in the fridge for up to 7 days.

orange blossom and honey dressing

makes ¾ cup (120 g)

This fragrant dressing, with a touch of sweetness from the honey, will add a level of sophistication to almost any salad. It's a handy dressing to keep on hand and use on the spur of the moment. It pairs particularly well with a mix of leafy greens, along with dried or fresh fruits, nuts, and soft white cheese such as feta.

- 3 tablespoons (45 g) olive oil
- 2 tablespoons (30 g) fresh lemon juice
- 1½ tablespoons (33 g) honey
- 2 teaspoons orange blossom water
- Large pinch of fine sea salt

1 Combine the olive oil, lemon juice, honey, orange blossom water, and salt in a small bowl and stir with a fork or a small whisk until well blended and smooth. The dressing can be stored in a sealed container in the fridge for up to 3 days; stir before using it.

caramelized tomatoes–maticha maasla

makes 1½ cups (320 g)

Although it doesn't have the same smooth texture as ketchup, I like to think of this, known as "maticha" in Arabic, as the Moroccan–improved!–version. And I think it should be used just as such: a powerful tart-sweet condiment.

- Pinch of saffron threads (5 or 6 threads), or substitute ½ teaspoon ground turmeric
- 2 tablespoons (30 g) warm water if using saffron
- 2 tablespoons (30 g) olive oil
- 1 pound (454 g) cherry tomatoes, halved lengthwise
- 1½ teaspoons honey
- ¾ teaspoon fine sea salt, or more to taste

1 If using saffron, combine the saffron threads and warm water in a small bowl and set aside.

2 Meanwhile, combine the olive oil, tomatoes, honey, and salt in a large frying pan and cook over medium-high heat, stirring occasionally, for about 7 minutes.

3 Add the saffron water or turmeric and cook until the water has evaporated and the tomatoes start to blister, 3 to 5 minutes. Reduce the heat to low and cook, stirring occasionally, until the tomatoes have broken down into a thick, chunky sauce, 25 to 30 minutes. Taste and adjust the seasoning, adding more salt, if desired. Remove from the heat and set aside to cool.

4 The caramelized tomatoes can be stored in a sealed container in the fridge for up to 5 days; bring to room temperature before serving.

almond, honey, and argan oil paste–amlou

makes ¾ cup (205 g)

Known as "amlou" in Morocco, this is a popular spread or dip made of almond butter, argan oil, and honey. You will always find it on a typical Moroccan breakfast table, next to freshly baked batbout (20-Minute Panfried Bread, page 86), plain m'semen (Garlic Butter and Cheese Flatbreads, page 75), or various pastries. Although it's traditionally prepared with almonds, it's not uncommon to come across versions made with peanut butter instead of almond butter, or a combination of both.

- ½ cup (120 g) natural (ideally roasted) almond butter, or substitute peanut butter
- 2½ tablespoons (55 g) honey
- 2 tablespoons (30 g) argan oil, or substitute walnut or peanut oil
- Generous pinch of fine sea salt

1 Combine the nut butter, honey, argan oil, and salt in a small container or a jar and stir together until well blended. Tightly seal the container or jar and store in a cool, dark, dry place, such as your kitchen cupboard, for up to 1 month.

olive, preserved lemon, and cilantro salsa

makes ½ cup (140 g)

This salsa is salty, herby, and briny in the best way. Serve it with tortilla chips, spoon it over any tagine or grilled foods, or use it in sandwiches.

- ⅓ cup (45 g) pitted green or purple olives, finely chopped
- ¼ cup (60 g) olive oil
- 1 to 2 tablespoons (20 to 40 g) seeded and finely chopped preserved lemons, homemade (page 41) or store-bought
- 3 tablespoons (18 g) finely chopped cilantro leaves and tender stems
- Fine sea salt, if needed

1 Combine the olives, olive oil, preserved lemons, and cilantro and mix well. Taste and add salt if necessary (the salsa may not need any, because the olives and preserved lemons are salty).

green pepper and tomato salsa—chlada tazia

makes 2 cups (500 g)

In Moroccan Arabic, the word "chlada" means "salad," and it most often refers to a small dish of raw or cooked vegetables served with bread as an appetizer. This preparation, which I refer to as Green Pepper and Tomato Salsa, has various names in Morocco: chlada tazia, chlada mechouia, and chlada ghiyatiya. To make it, green peppers—traditionally hot ones—tomatoes, and garlic are grilled until charred before being chopped and seasoned simply with extra-virgin olive oil and salt. It's another of those recipes that remind me how humble ingredients can be used to create truly special combinations. I usually make a big batch of it that can be enjoyed throughout the week alongside tagines, as a filling in sandwiches, or as a dipping sauce with tortilla chips.

You can roast the peppers, tomatoes, and garlic on an outdoor grill or stovetop griddle or use the broiler.

- 1 pound (453 g) Anaheim, poblano, or serrano chiles or green bell peppers (see Tip)
- 4 medium tomatoes (400 g), preferably Roma or San Marzano
- 3 garlic cloves (unpeeled)
- 3 tablespoons (45 g) olive oil
- ½ teaspoon fine sea salt, or more to taste

1 *To use a grill or griddle pan*: Prepare a hot fire in an outdoor grill or preheat a griddle over high heat. Place the peppers, tomatoes, and garlic on the grill or griddle. Grill the peppers and tomatoes for 3 to 4 minutes on each side, using tongs to turn them frequently, until the skin is charred on all sides and the flesh is starting to soften. Grill the garlic, turning once, for about 1 to 2 minutes on each side, until golden brown and soft. *Or, to use the oven broiler*: Set your broiler to its highest setting. Line a baking sheet with foil and arrange the peppers, tomatoes, and garlic on the pan. Broil the peppers and tomatoes, turning once, until the skin is charred and the flesh is starting to soften, 5 to 10 minutes. The timing will depend on the size of each vegetable: tomatoes and small peppers like poblano will take less time than green bell peppers. Broil the garlic, turning once, until golden brown and soft, about 3 minutes.

2 Once the peppers, tomatoes, and garlic are done, transfer them to a plastic bag and seal it. This will trap the steam and residual heat, allowing the vegetables, particularly the peppers, to continue cooking and making it easy to remove the skin.

3 Once they are cool enough to handle, use your hands or a butter knife to peel the peppers, tomatoes, and garlic. Remove the stems and seeds from the peppers, chop them into ¼- to ½-inch (0.6 to 1 cm) pieces, and transfer to a medium bowl. Roughly chop the tomatoes (no need to seed them) into pieces of the same size, reserving their juices, and transfer them, and the juices, to the bowl of chopped peppers. Peel the garlic, finely mince it, and stir into the peppers and tomatoes.

4 Add the olive oil and salt and stir to combine. Taste and adjust the seasoning, adding more salt if necessary. Serve, or refrigerate until ready to use. The salsa can be stored in a sealed container in the fridge for up to 5 days.

TIP: For a mild salsa, use only Anaheim peppers. For a hot one, use a mix of serranos and poblanos. And for a sweet salsa, use only bell peppers. Feel free to experiment with different combinations: for example, use Anaheim, poblano, and serrano peppers for a salsa with mild to medium heat, or add a green bell pepper to a salsa made with serranos for a touch of sweetness.

caramelized onions with raisins–t'faya

makes 1 cup (350 g)

T'faya is a classic relish made of caramelized onions and raisins cooked with honey and spices. While it's traditionally used to top couscous or tagines, adding a touch of sweetness, I love serving it with foods that are not so Moroccan: very sharp aged cheddar cheese or Gouda, for example, and crackers.

- 3 tablespoons (45 g) olive oil
- 2 large yellow onions (440 g), sliced
- ¾ cup (150 g) dark or golden raisins
- ¼ cup (60 g) vegetable stock or water
- 2 garlic gloves, minced or pressed
- 1½ tablespoons (33 g) honey
- ½ teaspoon ground cinnamon
- ½ teaspoon fine sea salt, or more to taste
- ⅛ teaspoon black pepper

1 Heat the olive oil in a large frying pan over medium-low heat. Add the onions, cover the pan, and cook, stirring occasionally, until the onions are soft and translucent and beginning to brown at the edges, 15 to 18 minutes.

2 Meanwhile, put the raisins in a small bowl and add boiling water to cover. Set aside to soak for 10 minutes, or until softened, then drain and set aside.

3 Add the stock or water, drained raisins, garlic, honey, cinnamon, salt and pepper to the pan, reduce the heat to low, and simmer, stirring occasionally, until the liquid has evaporated and the onions are golden brown, 20 to 25 minutes. Taste and adjust the seasoning, adding more salt if necessary. Remove from the heat.

4 This can be used immediately or refrigerated in a sealed container for up to 5 days; bring to room temperature before using.

فطور

BREAKFAST AND BRUNCH

lio

baked chermoula potatoes with eggs—batata m'chermla

serves 4

The name of this popular dish, batata m'chermla, translates as "potatoes in chermoula"—the signature marinade of Moroccan cuisine, usually made with cilantro, parsley, garlic, spices, lemon juice, and olive oil. This quick-and-easy version adds eggs for a delicious, stress-free Moroccan breakfast. The chermoula-marinated potatoes, crispy around the edges and soft on the inside, are served with eggs baked in the same pan just until the whites are set but the yolks are still runny.

- ¾ cup (150 g) Classic Chermoula (page 38)
- 1½ pounds (680 g) Yukon Gold or russet potatoes, peeled and cut into 1-inch (2.5 cm) pieces
- 1½ tablespoons (22 g) olive oil
- 4 large eggs
- ½ small red onion, finely chopped
- ½ cup (9 g) flat-leaf parsley leaves and tender stems, roughly chopped
- Hot sauce for serving, such as Harissa (page 44) or Cholula (optional)

1 Preheat the oven to 425°F (220°C). Put the chermoula and potatoes in a large bowl and toss to coat.

2 Drizzle the olive oil over the bottom of a baking sheet and use your hands or a pastry brush to spread it evenly over the pan. Arrange the potatoes in a single layer on the pan, leaving as much space as possible between them.

3 Bake the potatoes for 15 minutes. Remove the pan from the oven, flip the potatoes over with a spatula, and bake for another 10 to 15 minutes, until the potatoes are soft and the edges are starting to crisp up.

4 Move the potatoes around in the pan to make 4 spaces for the eggs and crack an egg into each space. Bake for 4 to 5 minutes, or until the egg whites are set but the yolks are still runny and the potatoes are crispy around the edges.

5 Scatter the red onion and parsley over the potatoes and eggs and serve immediately, with hot sauce, if desired.

semolina bread with salted honey butter–harcha

serves 4 to 6

Harcha is a bread traditionally made with coarse semolina flour. The word "harcha," which means "coarse" in Moroccan Arabic, refers to the texture of the bread or, more particularly, to the rough surface of its crust, the result of coating the dough with coarse semolina before baking. There are various forms of harcha in Morocco. The most common version is a thinner hand-shaped bread that is panfried, often sold in large or individual portions in bakeries. For another take, the dough is shaped into cookies that are flavored with orange zest and aniseed. Finally, there's an oven-baked version, which has become my favorite one to make at home over the years because it's totally foolproof and mostly hands-off. It has a coarse but still delicate crust, a moist interior, and a unique sweet, nutty flavor from the semolina flour. Warm harcha topped with honey butter is hard to resist, but feel free to serve it with your own favorite toppings, such as cream cheese or jam.

- 1 cup (180 g) semolina flour, preferably coarse, plus more for sprinkling
- 3 tablespoons (37 g) granulated sugar
- 1 teaspoon baking powder
- ½ teaspoon fine sea salt
- 4 tablespoons (56 g) unsalted butter, melted, plus more for the pan
- 2 tablespoons (30 g) olive oil
- ½ cup (120 g) milk, preferably whole milk
- 1 large egg

honey butter

- 8 tablespoons (113 g) unsalted butter, at room temperature
- ¼ cup (88 g) honey, or more to taste
- ⅛ to ¼ teaspoon fine sea salt (to taste)

1 Preheat the oven to 350°F (175°C). Whisk together the semolina flour, sugar, baking powder, and salt in a large bowl. Add the melted butter and olive oil and use your fingertips or a rubber spatula to combine them with the dry ingredients until the mixture looks like wet sand.

2 Whisk together the milk and egg in a small bowl. Add to the semolina mixture and stir until well combined. Cover the batter and let rest for 10 minutes to allow the semolina flour to absorb more of the liquid.

3 Grease an 8-inch (20 cm) cast-iron or other heavy ovenproof frying pan with butter. Sprinkle it generously with semolina flour, tilting the pan to coat the bottom evenly.

4 Transfer the batter to the prepared pan and spread it into an even layer with a spatula. Sprinkle semolina flour all over the top to coat the surface evenly.

5 Bake the harcha for 20 to 23 minutes, until golden, slightly risen, and springy to the touch; a toothpick inserted into the center should come out clean. Remove from the oven and let cool for about 5 minutes.

6 *While the harcha bakes, prepare the honey butter*: Mix the softened butter, honey, and salt in a small bowl until well combined. Taste and adjust the seasoning, adding more salt or honey if necessary.

7 When the harcha has cooled slightly, run a knife around the edges of the pan to loosen it. Carefully cut into slices (to avoid scratching the pan's surface). Alternatively, invert a large plate over the top of the pan and, using oven mitts to hold the pan and plate together, carefully flip them over to unmold the bread onto the plate.

8 Serve the harcha warm with the honey butter. The harcha can be stored in an airtight container at room temperature for up to 2 days.

sesame and aniseed brioche–krachel

makes 1 loaf

Krachel, Moroccan sweet rolls similar to brioche, hold a special place in my heart. Flavored with anise and sesame seeds, with a touch of orange blossom water, they transport me back to Fez and to the warm embrace of my maternal grandmother, Khadija, affectionately called Lalla Khadouch by her fifteen grandchildren. Whenever we visited her, she would serve these rolls, still warm from the oven, with butter, her homemade apricot jam, and a big pot of Moroccan mint tea. I used to find the aniseed overpowering, but to spare my grandmother's feelings, I'd put on a brave face and pretend to enjoy her krachel. Since then, I've come to appreciate the taste of anise, and now I often make this loaf version of classic krachel for my own family to enjoy.

- ½ cup (120 g) warm milk (110°F to 120°F / 43°C to 49°C)
- ¼ cup (50 g) granulated sugar
- 1½ teaspoons active dry yeast
- 4 cups (480 g) all-purpose flour, plus more for dusting
- 2½ tablespoons (25 g) toasted sesame seeds
- 2 teaspoons aniseed, roughly crushed using a mortar and pestle or briefly processed in a spice/coffee grinder, or 1 teaspoon ground anise
- 1 teaspoon fine sea salt
- 2 tablespoons (30 g) orange blossom water
- 3 large eggs, at room temperature
- 8 tablespoons (113 g) unsalted butter, at room temperature, plus more for the pan
- 1 egg, beaten with 1 tablespoon water, for egg wash
- 1 tablespoon sesame seeds, for sprinkling

1 In the bowl of a stand mixer, combine the warm milk and sugar and whisk or stir with a fork until the sugar has dissolved. Stir in the yeast and let the mixture sit for 5 minutes, or until foamy.

2 Mix together the flour, sesame seeds, aniseed, and salt in a medium bowl.

3 Attach the mixer bowl to the stand and fit the mixer with the dough hook. With the mixer on low speed, gradually add the flour mixture to the yeast and milk mixture, mixing just until combined. Add the orange blossom water, then add the eggs one at a time, mixing well after each addition and scraping down the sides of the bowl as needed. Continue mixing until the dough comes together, is elastic, and is still a bit sticky, about 10 minutes. If the dough isn't coming together or is still too sticky, add a little more flour 1 tablespoon at a time as necessary, mixing until incorporated.

(recipe continues)

4 With the mixer still on low speed, gradually add the butter, about 1 tablespoon at a time, making sure each addition is fully incorporated before adding more and scraping down the sides of the bowl as needed. Once all the butter has been incorporated (this will take about 5 minutes), increase the speed to medium-low and mix until the dough is smooth and elastic, about 5 minutes; it will still be a little bit tacky but it should not be sticky.

5 Transfer the dough to a large bowl, cover with a kitchen towel, and let rise in a warm place for 1 hour, or until it has doubled in size.

6 Butter an 8½-×-4½-inch (21 × 11 cm) loaf pan. Punch down the risen dough, turn it out onto a floured surface, and divide it into 8 pieces, then shape into balls. Arrange the balls in 2 rows in the loaf pan, cover with a kitchen towel, and let the dough rise again in a warm place for about 1 hour, until almost doubled in size.

7 Preheat the oven to 350°F (175°C). Gently brush the brioche loaf with the egg wash, making sure not to deflate the dough. Sprinkle sesame seeds generously over the top of the dough and bake for 30 to 35 minutes, or until the top is golden brown and a skewer inserted in the center of the loaf comes out clean.

8 Remove from the oven and let the brioche cool in the pan for 5 minutes, then transfer it to a wire rack to cool completely.

fried potato cakes with green pepper and tomato salsa—maakouda

serves 4

Maakouda, deep-fried potato cakes, are a popular Moroccan street food. Made from mashed potatoes seasoned with herbs and spices, the cakes are dipped in batter and fried until golden brown. Similarly to croquettes, they are crispy on the outside, soft and fluffy on the inside. They are the snack of choice for many Moroccans when wandering through the souks, often served with toppings and sauces inside a crispy baguette, making them very convenient to eat on the go. They can also be served on their own, as a side dish or a simple snack. When starting to cook the potato cakes, don't worry too much about creating perfectly shaped disks; once they hit the oil, they float back up to the surface, forming nicely shaped rounds on their own. The traditional topping is a sauce made of equal parts lemon juice and tomato paste, with some Harissa (page 44), but my favorite one is my Green Pepper and Tomato Salsa (page 50).

If you'd like to serve these at a party, you can shape the potato cakes in advance and then fry them shortly before serving.

potato cakes

- 1 pound (453 g) russet or Yukon Gold potatoes, peeled and cut into 1-inch (2.5 cm) pieces
- ½ cup (9 g) flat-leaf parsley leaves and tender stems, finely chopped
- 2 garlic cloves, minced or pressed
- 1½ teaspoons fresh lemon juice
- ¾ teaspoon fine sea salt, or more to taste
- ½ teaspoon ground cumin
- ½ teaspoon sweet paprika
- ¼ teaspoon black pepper
- About 4 cups (900 g) vegetable oil for deep-frying
- Flaky salt, such as Maldon, to serve (optional)

batter

- 1½ cups (180 g) all-purpose flour
- 1½ teaspoons baking powder
- 1 teaspoon active dry yeast
- ¾ teaspoon ground turmeric
- ½ teaspoon fine sea salt
- ¾ cup (180 g) warm water, plus more if needed
- 1½ tablespoons (22 g) vegetable oil

- 2 cups (500 g) Green Pepper and Tomato Salsa (page 50)

1 Fill a large pot with enough cold water to cover the potatoes by about 1 inch and bring to a boil. Carefully add the potatoes to the pot and bring the water back to a boil, then reduce the heat to medium-low and simmer, uncovered, until a fork slides easily into the potatoes, 10 to 13 minutes.

2 *While the potatoes cook, make the batter*: Whisk together the flour, baking powder, yeast, turmeric, and salt in a large bowl. Pour the warm water and vegetable oil over the dry ingredients and mix until you have a batter that has a consistency similar to pancake batter but is thick enough to coat the potato cakes. If necessary, add either more water or more flour, about ½ tablespoon at a time, until you obtain the right consistency. Cover the batter and let rest for at least 30 minutes, and up to 2 hours.

(recipe continues)

3 *Meanwhile, shape the potato cakes*: Drain the potatoes in a colander or sieve and let stand for 10 to 15 minutes, until thoroughly drained and dry.

4 Transfer the still-warm potatoes to a large bowl and use a potato masher or a fork to mash them until smooth. Add the parsley, garlic, lemon juice, salt, cumin, paprika, and pepper and mix well to combine. Taste and adjust the seasoning, adding more salt if necessary.

5 Divide the mixture into 14 equal portions (about 1½ tablespoons/30 g each) and form each one into a 2¼-inch (5.7 cm) disk. *(You can prepare the potato cakes up to 2 days in advance and store them in a sealed container or tightly covered with plastic wrap in the fridge until ready to cook.)*

6 Line a large plate or baking sheet with paper towels. Heat about 2 inches (5 cm) of oil in a deep 10-inch (25 cm) frying pan over medium heat until it reaches 350°F (175°C); a cube of bread dropped into the oil should brown in 30 seconds.

7 Give the batter a good stir. Working in batches of 3 or 4 to avoid crowding, place a potato cake in the batter, turning it with a large spoon to ensure it is fully coated on both sides, then gently lift it out with the spoon, allowing the excess batter to drip off, and transfer it to the hot oil; if desired, use another spoon to help slide the cake into the hot oil. Fry the potato cakes, until the undersides are golden, about 1 to 2 minutes, then carefully flip them and continue frying until both sides are golden and crisp, about 1 to 2 minutes. (Adjust the heat as necessary to maintain the oil temperature at around 350°F/175°C.) Using a slotted spoon, transfer the fried cakes to the lined plate or baking sheet to drain.

8 Let the potato cakes cool for about 5 minutes before serving with the salsa on the side. Finish with flaky salt, if desired.

TIP: Any leftover potato cakes can be stored in the fridge in a sealed container for up to 2 days. Reheat in a 350°F (175°C) oven for about 7 to 10 minutes, until heated through and crispy.

honey-buttered pancakes with orange blossom and blueberry sauce—baghrir

serves 4 to 6 (makes 12 pancakes)

Baghrir, made with a light semolina batter, are my favorite pancakes. With countless tiny holes all over their surface, they have a one-of-a-kind texture that is perfect for soaking up any topping you like. They are traditionally enjoyed with plain honey or a simple syrup of melted butter and honey. I like them with a blueberry sauce infused with orange blossom water, reminiscent of a classic American pancake topping.

You can cook the baghrir in advance and reheat them when needed. They keep very well in the freezer and are always welcome on busy mornings when you're short on time. And feel free to enjoy them with your favorite pancake topping instead of the blueberry sauce; my daughters love them with Nutella.

baghrir

- 1⅓ cups (240 g) semolina flour
- ⅓ cup (40 g) all-purpose flour
- 1 tablespoon granulated sugar
- 2 teaspoons baking powder
- 1¼ teaspoons active dry yeast
- ½ teaspoon fine sea salt
- 2 cups (480 g) warm water (110°F/43°C)

blueberry sauce (makes about 1¾ cups/400 g)

- ⅓ cup (80 g) water
- 1½ tablespoons fresh lemon juice, or more to taste
- 1½ teaspoons orange blossom water, or more to taste
- 1 tablespoon cornstarch
- 3 cups (390 g) fresh or frozen blueberries
- ¼ cup (50 g) granulated sugar

for serving

- 8 tablespoons (113 g) unsalted butter
- ½ cup (176 g) honey
- ⅓ cup (80 g) crème fraîche
- Grated lemon zest (optional)

1 *Make the baghrir:* Combine the semolina flour, all-purpose flour, sugar, baking powder, yeast, and salt in a blender, add the warm water, and blend until the batter is smooth, with no lumps. Alternatively, combine the ingredients in a large bowl and beat with a handheld electric mixer until smooth.

2 Check the consistency of the batter, as the results will depend on the coarseness of your semolina flour. The ideal consistency should be pourable but not watery, thinner than a traditional pancake batter, and slightly thicker than a traditional crêpe batter. If your batter seems too thick, add a little more warm water, 1 tablespoon at a time, as necessary. Conversely, if it's too runny, add a little more semolina flour, ½ tablespoon at a time, until it thickens.

3 Let the batter stand, covered, at room temperature for 25 minutes to allow the yeast to activate; the batter should be light and foamy, with lots of tiny bubbles. Blend or whisk again for a few seconds before cooking the pancakes.

(recipe continues)

4 *Meanwhile, make the blueberry sauce:* Whisk the water, lemon juice, orange blossom water, and cornstarch together in a medium saucepan until the cornstarch has dissolved. Stir in the blueberries and sugar and bring just to a simmer over medium-high heat. Reduce the heat to medium-low and cook, stirring occasionally, until the blueberries begin to soften and the sauce thickens slightly, about 5 minutes. Taste and adjust the seasoning, adding more orange blossom water and/or lemon juice, if desired. Remove from the heat and set aside; if desired, reheat the sauce over low heat before serving. *(The sauce can be made up to 5 days ahead, cooled, and refrigerated in a sealed container. Bring to room temperature or reheat gently before serving.)*

5 Set an 8-inch (20 cm) nonstick frying pan over medium-high heat and wait for it to get properly hot. (That will ensure that the batter sets properly and creates the pancake's characteristic holes.) Pour about ⅓ cup of batter into the center of the hot pan and allow it to spread into a circle; as soon as the batter hits the pan, plenty of small bubbles should appear all over the surface. (The pan doesn't require to be oiled, unless you're not using a nonstick pan). Once the pancake starts to set slightly and lose its sheen, within 60 to 90 seconds, it is ready (baghrir are cooked on one side only). Adjust the heat as necessary, keeping it between medium and medium-high. Transfer the pancake to a plate and repeat with the remaining batter, stacking the pancakes with sheets of parchment paper between them to prevent them from sticking together. *(The pancakes can be made ahead and stored in a sealed container or ziplock bag for up to 2 days in the fridge or up to 1 month in the freezer.)*

6 When ready to serve the pancakes, melt the butter in a large frying pan over medium heat. Add the honey and stir to combine, then reduce the heat to low. Add the pancakes to the pan two at a time, quickly turning them with a spatula to coat both sides with the syrup; don't let them soak in the syrup, or they will absorb too much of it. Arrange the pancakes on individual plates as you heat them and top each serving with a dollop of crème fraîche and blueberry sauce. If desired, garnish them with a sprinkling of lemon zest.

TIP: If only a few bubbles or only large bubbles appear when you add the batter to the pan, the pan may not be hot enough, or the batter may be too thick or hasn't proofed for long enough. In that case, add ¼ cup (60 g) warm water to the batter, blend or whisk again, and let proof for an additional 15 minutes, then proceed as directed.

preserved beef–express khlii

makes 2½ cups (540 g)

Moroccan khlii, pronounced "khlee," is meat that is marinated in a generous amount of garlic, cumin, coriander, and salt, then dried, traditionally in the sun, before being both cooked in and preserved in fat. The result is an unusual cross between beef jerky and beef confit. The classic version is sun-dried for days, but my "express" khlii, marinated for no more than 24 hours, delivers the signature flavors with a softer, moister texture. The most common way to enjoy khlii is with eggs for breakfast. Strips of the meat, along with some of the fat it's stored in, are heated in a small frying pan, then an egg is cracked into the pan and cooked until the white is set but the yolk is still runny. It's usually unnecessary to add salt to the eggs, as the meat itself is well seasoned. Khlii can also be added to dishes such as Loubia (page 82) or Adis (page 135) for an extra kick of flavor.

- 1½ pounds (680 g) boneless lean beef chuck, brisket, or boneless beef shank
- ⅓ cup (80 g) olive oil
- 5 garlic cloves, minced or pressed
- 2 tablespoons (14 g) ground coriander
- 2 teaspoons ground cumin
- 2 teaspoons fine sea salt
- 5 ounces (141 g) beef tallow, suet, or beef fat, cut into small chunks, or ½ cup (120 g) olive oil, plus more oil if necessary
- Fried eggs and tomato salad to serve (optional)

1 Cut the beef into thin strips about ¼ inch (0.6 cm) thick and 1 inch (2.5 cm) wide. If you have difficulty slicing the meat, place it in the freezer for about 15 minutes to firm up slightly.

2 Combine the olive oil, garlic, coriander, cumin, and salt in a large bowl and mix well. Add the beef and use your hands or a large spoon to coat it with the oil and spice mixture. Cover and marinate in the fridge overnight, or up to 24 hours.

3 Add the beef suet, tallow, or beef fat or the olive oil to a Dutch oven and heat over medium heat until melted. Add the marinated beef and cook, stirring occasionally, until fragrant, about 5 minutes.

4 Reduce the heat to low, cover the pot, and cook for 1½ to 2 hours, depending on the cut of beef, until it is tender and separates easily when pressed with a fork.

5 Remove the lid, increase the heat to medium-low, and cook, stirring occasionally, until all the moisture has evaporated and the beef strips look crispy, 25 to 45 minutes, again depending on the type of meat.

6 Serve immediately with fried eggs and tomato salad, if desired. Alternatively, carefully transfer the beef and fat to a jar or other container with a tight-fitting lid, making sure the meat is submerged in the fat; if necessary, top up with more olive oil to cover the meat. Let cool, then cover tightly and refrigerate.

7 The khlii will keep for up to 2 weeks in the fridge. Reheat briefly in a frying pan over medium-low heat before serving.

TIPS: You'll notice some small bits of meat mixed with fat at the bottom of the pot when your khlii is ready; don't discard them. Full of flavor and umami, these morsels and their fat are traditionally used to fill m'semen flatbreads (see the recipe for Garlic Butter and Cheese Flatbreads on page 75). I store them in a small container in the fridge and use them instead of butter in many savory preparations, from pasta sauces to soups or stews.

garlic butter and cheese flatbreads—m'semen

makes 10 flatbreads

The flaky semolina flatbreads known as m'semen are sold in bakeries and souks throughout Morocco, sometimes plain, sometimes stuffed with a mix of onions, bell peppers, and ground meat. The first time I made this version, I couldn't help but wonder why I hadn't thought of the combination sooner. The garlic-butter-and-cheese filling, made with lots of chopped parsley and cilantro, makes for an incredibly satisfying, herbaceous flatbread that's hard to resist. The number of steps in this recipe might seem daunting at first, but as soon as you start filling and folding the m'semen, you'll see that the preparation process quickly becomes intuitive, and the results are extremely rewarding.

To make plain m'semen, follow the recipe as instructed and skip the steps involving the herb-and-butter filling, as well as the cheese filling. To reheat leftover m'semen, warm them in a frying pan over medium heat, flipping them several times, until heated through, or heat on a baking sheet in a 350°F (175°C) oven for 3 to 5 minutes.

dough

- 3 cups (360 g) all-purpose flour
- 1 cup (180 g) semolina flour, plus more if needed
- 2 teaspoons granulated sugar
- 1 teaspoon baking powder
- 1 teaspoon fine sea salt
- 1¼ cups (300 g) warm water, plus more if needed
- Vegetable oil for coating the dough

for assembly

- 12 tablespoons (169 g) unsalted butter, melted
- ½ cup (120 g) vegetable oil, plus more for shaping the breads
- 6 garlic cloves, finely minced or pressed
- 1½ cups (27 g) flat-leaf parsley leaves and tender stems, finely chopped
- 1½ cups (27 g) cilantro leaves and tender stems, finely chopped
- ½ teaspoon granulated sugar
- 1 teaspoon fine sea salt
- ⅛ teaspoon black pepper
- 1 cup (112 g) grated cheddar cheese
- 1 cup (112 g) grated mozzarella cheese
- 5 tablespoons (56 g) semolina flour

(recipe continues)

1 *Make the dough*: In the bowl of a stand mixer or in a large bowl, mix together the flours, sugar, baking powder, and salt. Add the water and use a large spoon or a rubber spatula to mix with the flour and form a smooth dough. If the dough seems too dry, add a little more warm water 1 tablespoon at a time. Or, if it's still too sticky, gradually add a little more semolina flour 1 teaspoon at a time.

2 If using a stand mixer, switch to the dough hook and mix on low speed until the dough is smooth, supple, and elastic, about 10 minutes. Or, if making the dough by hand, transfer the dough to a clean work surface and knead until it is smooth, supple, and elastic, about 15 minutes. If the dough feels dry at any point, dip your fingers in water and then continue kneading.

3 Turn the dough out and coat with a bit of oil, then return to the bowl, cover, and let rest for 15 minutes.

4 Turn the dough out and divide it into 10 equal pieces. Form each piece into a ball and use your hands to coat each one with a little oil. Transfer the balls to a plate, cover with plastic wrap, and let rest for at least 30 minutes, and up to 2 hours. (The resting time allows the gluten to relax and will make the dough easier to stretch when you fold the m'semen.)

5 *Make the fillings*: Combine ½ cup (113 g) of the melted butter, 6 tablespoons (90 g) of the vegetable oil, the garlic, parsley, cilantro, sugar, salt, and pepper in a small bowl. Combine the remaining ¼ cup (56 g) melted butter and 2 tablespoons (30 g) vegetable oil in another small bowl. Combine the cheddar and mozzarella in a medium bowl, tossing to mix.

6 *Fill and fold the breads*: Oil a baking sheet and set aside. Keep the four bowls containing the fillings within reach: one with the butter-and-herb mixture, one with butter and oil, one with the cheeses, and the fourth with semolina flour. Generously oil your work surface and place one ball of dough on it. Flatten the ball slightly with your hands and spoon about ½ tablespoon of the butter and oil mixture on top of it. Using your hands, press the dough into a thin 11-inch (28 cm) circle or square; it's okay if the dough tears a little.

7 Drizzle about 1½ tablespoons of the herb and butter mixture over the dough and use your hands to spread it evenly over the dough. Sprinkle about 1½ teaspoons semolina flour over the dough, then, sprinkle 2½ to 3 tablespoons (17 to 21 g) of the cheese mixture evenly over the dough.

8 Fold the top third of the dough over toward the center, then fold the bottom third up over it, as if you were folding a business letter. Fold the left side of the dough over to the center and then fold the right side over it, to make a square about 2½ inches (6.3 cm) across. Place the folded m'semen seam side down on the prepared baking sheet and cover with a clean cloth or plastic wrap. Repeat with the remaining dough balls and filling.

9 *Cook the breads*: Heat a large, heavy-bottomed frying pan or a griddle over medium heat. Transfer one of the folded breads to a work surface and, using your hands, flatten it into a 5½-inch (14 cm) square. Gently place it in the hot pan and cook, turning several times and adjusting the heat as necessary, until golden on both sides and starting to puff, about 1½ to 2 minutes on each side. Transfer to a plate, cover with a clean towel to keep warm, and repeat with the remaining breads. Serve hot or warm.

amlou croissant bread pudding

serves 6

Amlou, a Moroccan spread (made with honey, almond butter and argan oil), and croissants are quintessential breakfast foods in their respective countries of origin. When the two are combined and transformed into a bread pudding, as in this recipe, the result is both unusual and delicious. I still don't know what I love more about this dish: the crispy bits of croissant filled with nutty, caramelized amlou at the surface of the pudding or the custardy ones at the bottom of the pan. It's a tough choice. While this pudding would usually be considered a breakfast or brunch dish, I enjoy it just as much for dessert.

8 croissants, ideally 2 days old
¾ cup (205 g) amlou (page 49)
2 cups (480 g) milk, preferably whole
1 cup (240 g) heavy cream
4 large eggs, beaten
2 teaspoons vanilla extract
⅔ cup (133 g) granulated sugar
2 teaspoons ground cinnamon
Large pinch of fine sea salt
½ cup (50 g) sliced almonds

1 Preheat the oven to 350°F (175°C). Grease a 9-×-13-inch (23 × 33 cm) baking dish. Use a serrated knife to make a lengthwise slit down the middle of each croissant. Fill each croissant with 2 tablespoons of the amlou and spread it evenly inside the croissant. Still using the serrated knife, cut the croissants into 1- to 1½-inch (2.5 to 3.8 cm) pieces and transfer them to the greased baking dish.

2 Combine the milk, heavy cream, eggs, vanilla extract, sugar, cinnamon, and salt in a large bowl and stir until well combined. Pour the mixture evenly over the croissant pieces. Scatter the sliced almonds over the top.

3 Bake the pudding for 45 to 50 minutes, until the custard is set, the edges of the croissant pieces at the surface are crispy, and the sliced almonds are golden. If the pudding starts to brown too much before it is done, tent it loosely with foil. Let cool for 10 to 15 minutes before serving.

avocado and almond smoothie–zaazaa

serves 4

Zaazaa is a Moroccan smoothie made from avocados and almonds, often sweetened with honey and enriched with dried fruits, that is enjoyed for breakfast or as a nourishing afternoon snack. It's commonly sold in mahlabas, bustling shops specializing in fresh dairy products including yogurt, smoothies, juices, and pastries. Zaazaa is highly customizable, but while some add their favorite cookies or chocolate or bananas to the mix, I prefer a slightly refined version with just a touch of floral orange blossom water. You can adjust the sweetness with more honey or maple syrup, and add dried fruits if you like. Similarly, the texture can be easily adjusted to personal taste by adjusting the amount of milk.

- 2 ripe avocados
- 1 cup (240 g) ice cubes
- ⅔ cup (94 g) raw almonds
- 6 pitted dates
- 2½ cups (600 g) milk, preferably whole, plus more if desired
- 2 tablespoons (44 g) honey or maple syrup, or more to taste
- 1½ tablespoons orange blossom water, or more to taste
- Pinch of ground cinnamon (optional)
- Grated chocolate and chopped almonds for garnish (optional)

1 Cut the avocados in half, remove the pits, and use a large spoon to scoop the flesh into a blender. Add the ice cubes, almonds, dates, milk, honey or maple syrup, orange blossom water, and cinnamon, if using, and blend until smooth and creamy. Taste and add more honey or maple syrup and/or more orange blossom water, if desired. Add more milk, if desired, for a thinner consistency and blend briefly.

2 Pour the smoothie into four glasses. If desired, garnish with chopped almonds and grated chocolate.

beans on toast with harissa oil—loubia

serves 4

Loubia is a comforting dish of cannellini beans simmered in a rich tomato sauce with onions and aromatic spices. My mom cooked it regularly for us when we were growing up in Brussels. She sometimes added warm crumbled pieces of khlii (see Preserved Beef, page 73), to her loubia for a meaty, umami kick. Having lived in London for many years, I have naturally embraced the British habit of eating beans on toast, a classic breakfast dish, though I prefer it for lunch or supper. Morocco has a tradition of enjoying beans with bread, so serving loubia on toast feels very natural.

- 3 tablespoons (45 g) olive oil
- 1 small onion (120 g), finely chopped
- 2 garlic cloves, minced or pressed
- 1 tablespoon (15 g) tomato paste
- 1½ teaspoons sweet paprika
- 1 teaspoon ground cumin
- 1 teaspoon ground turmeric
- 1 teaspoon ground ginger
- 3 medium tomatoes (300 g), halved and grated on the large holes of a box grater, or finely chopped, with their juices (alternatively, use about two-thirds of a 14.5-ounce can of diced tomatoes)
- ⅔ cup (160 g) vegetable stock, plus more if needed
- ½ cup flat-leaf parsley leaves and tender stems, finely chopped, plus more for garnish
- ¾ teaspoon fine sea salt, or more to taste
- Two 15-ounce (425 g) cans cannellini beans, drained and rinsed

harissa oil

- 3 tablespoons (45 g) olive oil
- 1 tablespoon (22 g) harissa, homemade (page 44) or store-bought

- 4 large slices bread of your choice
- Olive oil for drizzling

1 Heat the olive oil in a large frying pan over medium-low heat. Add the onion, garlic, tomato paste, paprika, cumin, turmeric, and ginger and cook, stirring occasionally, until fragrant, 1 to 2 minutes.

2 Add the tomatoes and their juices, the stock, parsley, and salt and bring to a simmer. Cover the pan, reduce the heat to low, and simmer for 35 to 40 minutes, until the sauce is fragrant, its texture is more velvety, and it has slightly reduced; stir every to 10 to 15 minutes to prevent the sauce from sticking to the bottom of the pan.

3 Add the beans and stir to coat. If the tomato sauce is too thick to coat the beans well, add a few tablespoons of stock or water. Cover the pan and cook until the beans are warm and tender, 10 to 15 minutes.

4 *Meanwhile, make the harissa oil*: Combine the olive oil and harissa in a small bowl and mix well.

5 Heat a large frying pan or griddle over medium heat. Drizzle the slices of bread with olive oil, add to the hot pan, and toast, turning once, until golden brown on both sides, about 2 minutes. Remove from the heat.

6 Arrange the toast on plates, top with the beans, drizzle with the harissa oil, sprinkle with chopped parsley, and serve.

brown butter semolina porridge with sesame nut crunch—assida

serves 4 to 6

Known as assida in Morocco, this semolina porridge is served at special occasions and religious festivals in Morocco, such as Eid al Mawlid, which commemorates the birth of the Prophet Muhammad. With its smooth, comforting texture, it is typically served warm for breakfast, topped with butter and honey. I have many fond memories of my cousins and me enjoying bowls of assida and playfully arguing over the honey jar as we were growing up. For this more sophisticated version, I make brown butter and add the butter and honey directly to the creamy porridge, infusing it with rich, nutty, sweet notes. Then I finish it all off with a crunchy topping of sesame seeds and nuts.

- 1⅓ cups (240 g) semolina flour, preferably coarse
- 5⅓ cups (1280 g) warm water
- 8 tablespoons (113 g) unsalted butter

sesame nut crunch

- 2 tablespoons (22 g) peanuts, roughly chopped or crushed
- 2 tablespoons (20 g) pistachios, chopped or crushed
- 3 tablespoons (30 g) toasted sesame seeds
- 1 tablespoon brown sugar
- ⅛ teaspoon fine sea salt
- Large pinch of ground cinnamon

- ⅓ cup (117 g) honey, or more to taste
- ⅓ cup (66 g) granulated sugar
- ¼ teaspoon fine sea salt

1 Stir together the semolina flour and warm water in a medium pot and cook over medium heat, stirring frequently with a heatproof spatula, until the mixture starts to thicken and comes to a boil, about 5 minutes. Reduce the heat to low and cook, stirring occasionally, until the semolina is tender and cooked through, 10 to 13 minutes.

2 *Meanwhile, make the brown butter*: Melt the butter in a small saucepan over medium heat and then continue to cook, swirling the pan occasionally for even cooking, until the butter turns golden brown and develops a nutty aroma, 5 to 7 minutes; be careful not to let it burn. Remove from the heat and set aside.

3 *Make the nut crunch*: Combine the peanuts, pistachios, sesame seeds, brown sugar, salt, and cinnamon in a small bowl. Set aside.

4 Add the brown butter, honey, sugar, and salt to the cooked semolina and stir to combine, then taste and add more honey, if desired.

5 Ladle the warm porridge into shallow bowls and sprinkle about 1 tablespoon of the sesame nut crunch on top of each one. Serve immediately.

TIP: Any leftover porridge can be stored in a sealed container in the fridge for up to 3 days. Reheat gently before serving.

20-minute panfried bread–quick batbout

makes four 6-inch (15 cm) flatbreads

Batbout is a panfried flatbread that combines elements of pita and naan yet has its own distinctive characteristics. What truly sets it apart is the semolina flour used both in the dough and for dusting the flatbreads, resulting in a unique texture: slightly grainy on the outside, soft and pillowy on the inside. This quick version of batbout allows you to have delicious warm, fresh flatbreads in minutes. Use the breads for dipping into spreads or to soak up the juices of a tagine, or make sandwiches with them.

- 1¼ cups (150 g) all-purpose flour, plus more if needed
- ⅔ cup (120 g) semolina flour, plus more for dusting
- 2 teaspoons baking powder
- 1 teaspoon granulated sugar
- ¾ teaspoon fine sea salt
- 1 cup (226 g) whole-milk yogurt
- 1½ tablespoons (22 g) olive oil

1 Combine the all-purpose flour, semolina flour, baking powder, sugar, and salt in a large bowl and mix together with a whisk or fork. Add the yogurt and olive oil and use a rubber spatula to start mixing the dough; when it becomes too stiff to stir, use your hands to bring the ingredients together, then form the dough into a ball.

2 Lightly dust a work surface with semolina flour, turn the dough out, and knead it for 3 to 5 minutes, until smooth and just lightly sticky. If the dough is too sticky, knead in a little more all-purpose flour ½ tablespoon at a time; if it's too dry, add a little bit of water ½ tablespoon at a time. Divide the dough into 4 equal pieces and roll each one into a ball.

3 Heat a large cast-iron or other heavy frying pan or a griddle over medium heat. While the pan is preheating, dust your worktop with more semolina flour and, using a rolling pin, roll each piece of dough into a 6-inch (15 cm) disk about ¼ inch (0.6 cm) thick.

4 Lightly dust the top of one disk with semolina flour and transfer to the hot pan. Cook for a few minutes on each side, until the bread turns lightly golden in spots and puffs up. Remove from the pan and wrap in a kitchen towel to keep warm while you cook the remaining breads; wipe out any excess semolina flour from the pan before adding another disk of dough.

TIP: To speed up the process, use two pans and work in batches of two, rolling out the second batch of dough while the first breads cook.

soft cheese–j'ben

makes 1¾ cups (14 ounces/400 g)

J'ben is Morocco's national white cheese. This creamy fresh cheese has a light tang and is subtly sweet. While it's a challenge to find j'ben outside of Morocco, it's very simple to make at home and requires just a few ingredients. Making it is very similar to making fresh ricotta, but unlike ricotta, j'ben contains buttermilk. It is often enjoyed simply on its own as a spread for flatbreads like batbout (see 20-Minute Panfried Bread, page 86) or m'semen (see Garlic Butter and Cheese Flatbreads, page 75), but my favorite way to eat it is spread over warm toasted bread, drizzled generously with honey, and finished with a sprinkle of chile flakes and a dash of flaky salt. You can also mix j'ben with chopped fresh herbs, lemon zest, and salt for a vibrant spread for bread or toast.

You can substitute j'ben anywhere you'd use fresh ricotta—for example, in sandwiches, sauces, or desserts.

- 3 cups (720 g) whole milk
- ⅔ cup (150 g) heavy cream
- 3 cups (750 g) buttermilk
- 1 tablespoon (15 g) fresh lemon juice
- 2 teaspoons fine sea salt

1 Pour the milk and cream into a large pot and heat over medium-high heat until the mixture reaches 190°F (90°C). If you don't have a thermometer, this will be just below a simmer; you will see steam rising from the surface and small bubbles forming around the edges of the pot.

2 Immediately stir in the buttermilk, lemon juice, and salt. Reduce the heat to medium-low and leave the mixture untouched until it separates into curds and whey (transparent liquid)—this shouldn't take more than 2 or 3 minutes. Turn off the heat and let the mixture stand for 15 minutes.

3 Line a fine-mesh sieve with cheesecloth or a kitchen towel and set over a deep bowl. Carefully and slowly pour the warm milk mixture into the sieve, then set aside to drain for at least 2 hours. The longer it drains, the firmer the cheese will be once chilled. (For a quicker route, instead of draining the cheese, you can grab the edges of the cheesecloth or towel and squeeze out as much liquid as possible.)

4 Transfer the drained cheese to a sealed container and refrigerate for at least 1 hour before serving; the cheese will keep, refrigerated, for up to 5 days.

ⵜⴰⵏⴰⴳⴰ
سلطة

SALADS AND SMALL VEGETABLE PLATES

CAN JOIN THE
26
186832

cumin and parsley potato salad

serves 4

Most Moroccan households have their favorite way of preparing this classic potato salad. It usually features a vibrant combination of fresh herbs like parsley, crunchy raw onions, and warm spices including cumin or paprika, all brought together with a zingy lemon juice or vinegar dressing. This recipe is my own favorite way to make the salad, although you can substitute cilantro for the parsley, if you prefer. More than a simple side, this is usually served as an appetizer, but it also works beautifully with other dishes such as Beef Skewers with Dill and Lemon Chermoula (page 187) and Chermoula Salmon with Quick-Pickled Cucumbers (page 223).

Good-quality white wine vinegar is key to the flavor of the potato salad; I recommend opting for the best you can find.

- 1½ pounds (680 g) yellow or red baby potatoes, or a mix (not peeled)
- Large pinch of fine sea salt
- ⅓ cup (80 g) olive oil
- 2 teaspoons ground cumin
- 2 tablespoons (30 g) white wine vinegar
- 1 teaspoon fine sea salt
- 1 medium red onion (170 g), finely sliced
- 1 cup (18 g) flat-leaf parsley leaves and tender stems, finely chopped

1 Put the potatoes in a large pot and cover them with cold water. Add a large pinch of salt to the water and bring to a boil over high heat. Reduce the heat to medium-low and simmer until the potatoes are tender when pierced with a knife, 10 to 15 minutes. Drain the potatoes and let cool slightly, then quarter or halve them, depending on size while they are still warm.

2 While the potatoes are cooking, heat the olive oil in a small skillet over medium heat. Add the cumin and cook, stirring frequently, until fragrant, 1 to 2 minutes. Remove from the heat, cover, and set the oil aside until ready to use.

3 Combine the cumin-infused olive oil, white wine vinegar, and 1 teaspoon salt in a large bowl and stir until well combined. Add the warm potatoes, red onions, and parsley to this marinade and gently toss until the potatoes are evenly coated. Taste and adjust the seasoning, adding more salt if necessary.

4 Serve the potato salad at room temperature or chilled. (The salad can be stored in the fridge in a sealed container for up to 3 days.)

peach and tomato salad with orange blossom and honey dressing

serves 4

This salad is my idea of a summer party on a plate. The sweetness of the peaches and the tanginess of the tomatoes are beautifully complemented by a fragrant orange blossom dressing. If peaches are not in season, the recipe also works nicely with wedges of apple or pear, or slices of mango. I love to pair it with Sticky Orange and Turmeric Chicken Skewers (page 156) or grilled seafood.

- 1½ cups (225 g) halved cherry tomatoes or Roma tomatoes cut into 1-inch (2.5 cm) chunks
- Half a small red onion (60 g), thinly sliced
- 2 cups (50 g) arugula
- ½ cup (9 g) cilantro leaves and tender stems, roughly torn
- ½ cup (9 g) flat-leaf parsley leaves and tender stems, roughly torn
- 2 peaches, halved, pitted, and sliced into ½-inch-thick (1.2 cm) wedges
- Fine sea salt and black pepper
- 3 tablespoons (22 g) pumpkin seeds
- ½ cup (75 g) crumbled feta
- ¾ cup (120 g) Orange Blossom and Honey Dressing (page 48)

1 Transfer the tomatoes and sliced onion to a bowl, toss gently, and set aside until ready to use. *(You can prepare these ahead and keep them, covered, in a cool place or the fridge for several hours.)*

2 When ready to serve, toss together the arugula, cilantro, and parsley on a large serving plate. Top with the tomatoes and onion, along with the peaches. Sprinkle with salt and pepper. Garnish the salad with the pumpkin seeds and crumbled feta, drizzle the dressing over the top, and serve immediately.

orange and black-olive radicchio salad

serves 4 to 6

In Morocco, we're fortunate to have an abundance of sweet, flavorful oranges. They often find their way into desserts, of course, but also into refreshing salads, marrying beautifully with savory ingredients. Here, the sweetness and tanginess of the oranges are balanced with the slightly bitter notes of the black olives and radicchio, the crunch of nuts, and a hint of cilantro. I love how the salad both brings a burst of color to the table and offers an unusual but delicious mix of textures and flavors.

- ½ cup (60 g) chopped walnuts
- 4½ tablespoons (67 g) olive oil
- 3 tablespoons (45 g) red wine vinegar
- 1½ tablespoons (33 g) honey
- 1 teaspoon dried oregano
- ¼ teaspoon fine sea salt, or to taste
- Large pinch of black pepper
- 1 medium head radicchio (340 g), quartered lengthwise, halved crosswise, and leaves separated
- 2 large oranges (453 g), peeled and cut into ¼-inch-thick (0.6 cm) slices, seeds removed
- 1 small red onion (120 g), thinly sliced
- ½ cup (70 g) pitted cured or dried black olives, halved lengthwise
- 1 cup (18 g) cilantro leaves and tender stems

1 Toast the chopped walnuts in a small frying pan over medium heat, stirring frequently, until fragrant and lightly golden brown, about 3 minutes. Remove from the heat and set aside.

2 Combine the olive oil, vinegar, honey, oregano, salt, and pepper in a small bowl and whisk until thoroughly combined and emulsified.

3 Combine the radicchio, orange slices, red onions, olives, cilantro, and toasted walnuts in a large bowl and toss well.

4 Whisk the dressing again, pour over the salad, and toss to coat. Transfer to a large serving plate or individual plates and serve.

harissa caesar salad with crispy spiced chickpeas

serves 4

This is my Moroccan-inspired version of the ever-popular Caesar salad. The harissa in the dressing adds smoky heat that works well against the creamy richness and tanginess of the dressing, and the spiced crispy chickpeas, like croutons, provide a satisfying crunch. This salad is a hit every time I serve it, whether at home or for special events. It's great for potlucks or a light lunch, or serve it alongside grilled meats or roasted vegetables.

crispy chickpeas

- One 15-ounce (425 g) can chickpeas, drained and rinsed
- 1½ tablespoons cornstarch
- 2 tablespoons (30 g) olive oil
- 1 teaspoon ground cumin
- 1 teaspoon sweet paprika
- ½ teaspoon fine sea salt, or more to taste
- ¼ teaspoon granulated sugar

harissa caesar dressing

- 1 cup (220 g) mayonnaise
- ½ cup (80 g) grated Parmesan cheese
- 2 tablespoons (30 g) fresh lemon juice
- 1 tablespoon (22 g) harissa, homemade (page 44) or store-bought, or more to taste
- 4 anchovy fillets, minced, or 1 teaspoon anchovy paste
- 1 teaspoon Dijon mustard
- 1 teaspoon Worcestershire sauce
- ¼ teaspoon fine sea salt, or more to taste
- ¼ teaspoon black pepper
- ¼ teaspoon granulated sugar

- 4 small (or 2 large) hearts of romaine (1¼ pounds/566 g)
- 2 tablespoons (20 g) grated Parmesan cheese

1 *Make the chickpeas*: Preheat the oven to 400°F (205°C). Line a baking sheet with parchment paper.

2 Dry the chickpeas thoroughly with a clean kitchen towel or paper towels and transfer to a large bowl. Sprinkle the cornstarch over the chickpeas and toss until evenly coated. Drizzle the olive oil over the chickpeas and toss to coat.

3 Spread the chickpeas out on the prepared baking sheet and bake for 30 to 35 minutes, until golden brown and crispy. Shake the pan to move the chickpeas around halfway through for even browning.

4 Remove the chickpeas from the oven and transfer to a medium bowl. Add the cumin, paprika, salt, and sugar and toss well until the chickpeas are evenly coated with the spices. Taste and add more salt if necessary. Let the chickpeas cool, then store in an airtight container at room temperature for up to 2 days.

5 *Make the dressing*: Combine the mayonnaise, Parmesan cheese, lemon juice, harissa, anchovies, mustard, Worcestershire sauce, salt, pepper, and sugar in a medium bowl and stir well. Taste and add more salt and/or harissa, if desired. Transfer to a jar or other covered container and refrigerate until ready to serve. *(It can be stored in the fridge for up to 3 days.)*

6 When ready to serve, cut the romaine hearts lengthwise in half, or into quarters if using large ones. Transfer to a large bowl, pour the dressing over the lettuce, and use tongs or your hands to gently coat the romaine leaves with the dressing.

7 Transfer to a large serving plate, scatter the chickpeas over the romaine, sprinkle with the Parmesan, and serve.

spiced carrots with almonds, olives, and herbs

serves 4

This dish is my culinary ode to one of the most underappreciated heroes of the kitchen, the carrot: tender, caramelized roasted carrots, bathed in a fragrant blend of spices and zesty harissa and finished with a topping of chopped green olives, almonds, and parsley, all served on a bed of cooling Greek yogurt. The almonds add crunch, while the briny notes of the olives introduce a somewhat surprising twist. This recipe is always a winner at my dinner parties.

3 tablespoons (45 g) olive oil, plus more for drizzling
1 tablespoon honey (22 g)
1 to 2 tablespoons (22 to 44 g) harissa, homemade (page 44) or store-bought
3 garlic cloves, minced or pressed
1 tablespoon tomato paste
1 tablespoon water
1 teaspoon ground cumin
1 teaspoon sweet paprika
½ teaspoon fine sea salt
1 pound (453 g) medium carrots, halved lengthwise and cut into 3-inch (7.6 cm) pieces

olive, almond, and herb topping

1 tablespoon olive oil
1½ teaspoons white wine vinegar
¼ teaspoon granulated sugar, or more to taste
Generous pinch of fine sea salt, or more to taste
1 cup (140 g) pitted green olives, roughly chopped
½ cup (65 g) roasted almonds, roughly chopped
½ cup (9 g) flat-leaf parsley leaves and tender stems, roughly chopped

1½ cups (360 g) Greek yogurt
½ teaspoon fine sea salt

1 *Make the carrots:* Preheat the oven to 425°F (220°C). Combine the olive oil, honey, harissa, garlic, tomato paste, water, cumin, paprika, and salt together in a large bowl and stir well. Add the carrots and toss until well coated.

2 Spread the carrots out on a baking sheet, leaving space between them so they will roast and char rather than steam. Cover the pan with foil and roast the carrots for 20 minutes, or until tender. Remove the foil and roast for another 10 minutes, or until the carrots have caramelized and started to brown in spots. Remove from the oven and set aside. You can serve the carrots warm or at room temperature.

3 *Meanwhile, make the topping*: Stir together the olive oil, vinegar, sugar, and salt in a medium bowl. Add the olives, almonds, and parsley, tossing to mix, then taste and adjust the seasoning, adding more salt or sugar if necessary. *(You can prepare the topping up to 4 hours in advance and store in a sealed container in the fridge; bring to room temperature before serving.)*

4 To serve, mix the yogurt with the salt and spread on a large serving plate or individual plates. Arrange the carrots on top of the yogurt and scatter the topping over them. Drizzle olive oil over the carrots and serve immediately.

TIP: To make this dish vegan, use nondairy yogurt.

green beans in garlicky oil—"bil zeit"

serves 4

"Bil zeit," which translates as "with oil" in Arabic, refers to the generous amount of olive oil flavored with garlic, cilantro, and spices. Usually this dish is prepared with fresh fava beans, but since they're not always easily available, I've found that green beans make a very good substitute. In Morocco, this is typically served as a starter along with other dishes like zaalouk (see Eggplant Dip with Red Bell Pepper, page 106) or bakoula (see the headnote to "Bakoula" Greens Galette with Burrata, page 125), but it also makes a fantastic accompaniment to roasted fish or grilled meats. Be sure to serve it with plenty of bread for dipping into the sauce.

- 1/4 cup (60 g) olive oil
- 4 garlic cloves, minced or pressed
- 2 teaspoons sweet paprika
- 1 1/2 teaspoons ground cumin
- 2 medium tomatoes (200 g), halved and grated on the large holes of a box grater, or finely chopped, with their juices (alternatively, use about half of a 14.5-ounce can of diced tomatoes)
- 1/2 cup (120 g) vegetable stock or water
- 1 cup (18 g) cilantro leaves and tender stems, finely chopped
- 3/4 teaspoon fine sea salt, or more to taste
- 1/8 teaspoon granulated sugar
- 1 pound (453 g), green beans, stem ends trimmed
- Two 1/2-inch-thick (1.2 cm) lemon slices

1 Heat the olive oil in a large frying pan over medium heat. Add the garlic, paprika, and cumin and cook, stirring occasionally, until fragrant, about 2 minutes.

2 Add the tomatoes, stock or water, cilantro, salt, and sugar and stir to combine. Add the green beans and lemon slices and stir to coat. Bring to a boil over high heat, then cover the pan, reduce the heat to medium-low, and simmer until the green beans start to soften, 8 to 12 minutes.

3 Remove the lid and cook until the green beans are tender and the sauce has reduced, about 5 minutes. Taste and adjust the seasoning, adding more salt if necessary.

4 Transfer to a large serving plate and serve hot.

eggplant dip with red bell pepper–zaalouk

serves 4 (makes 3½ cups/900 g)

Zaalouk is the simple but utterly delicious way Moroccans transform the humble eggplant. It is one of many "cooked salads" in the Moroccan repertoire, often served as a dip to kick off a meal. The eggplant can be baked, steamed, deep-fried, or simply cooked on the stovetop, as in this recipe. Here it is simmered with tomatoes, spices, and herbs, giving it an aromatic kick and an irresistible melt-in-your-mouth texture; for this version, I've included red bell peppers, which add subtle sweetness. My favorite way to enjoy zaalouk when I was a child was spread on a split crusty baguette that my mom would fill with kefta meatballs and ketchup. Today I swap harissa for the ketchup and add labneh (thick drained Middle Eastern yogurt), but that sandwich is still one of my favorite ways to eat zaalouk.

- 3 tablespoons (45 g) olive oil, plus more for drizzling
- 2 medium Italian eggplants or 2 small globe eggplants (680 g), chopped into 1-inch (2.5 cm) chunks (not peeled)
- 2 medium red bell peppers (280 g), cored, seeded, and cut into ½-inch (1.2 cm) pieces
- 4 medium tomatoes (400 g), halved and grated on the large holes of a box grater, or finely chopped, with their juices (alternatively, use a 14.5-ounce can of diced tomatoes)
- 2 tablespoons (12 g) finely chopped cilantro leaves and tender stems, plus a handful of roughly chopped cilantro for garnish
- 1 tablespoon tomato paste
- 1 teaspoon honey, or more to taste
- 3 garlic cloves, minced or pressed
- 2 teaspoons sweet paprika
- 1½ teaspoons ground cumin
- 1 teaspoon fine sea salt, or more to taste
- Fresh lemon juice (optional)

1 Heat the olive oil in a large frying pan over medium heat until hot. Add the eggplant, bell pepper, tomatoes, cilantro, tomato paste, honey, garlic, paprika, cumin, and salt. Cover the pan, reduce the heat to medium-low, and cook, stirring occasionally to make sure the vegetables don't stick to the bottom of the pan, for about 25 minutes, or until they are soft.

2 Remove the lid and crush the vegetables with a potato masher or the back of a large wooden spoon. Increase the heat to medium and cook, stirring occasionally, until all the liquid in the pan has evaporated, 5 to 8 minutes. Taste and adjust the seasoning, adding more honey and/or salt, or a little lemon juice, if desired.

3 Serve the zaalouk warm or at room temperature, garnished with chopped cilantro and a drizzle of olive oil. (The zaalouk can be kept in the fridge in a sealed container for up to 3 days.)

triple-lemon charred broccolini with breadcrumbs

serves 4 to 6

Broccolini isn't the most popular green (especially among young children like mine), but like other underrated vegetables, if it is cooked and seasoned properly, it can become a real treat. Here the broccolini is charred, turning it crispy on the edges and tender on the inside; the process also gives it a sweeter, caramelized flavor. The seasoning of lemon juice, lemon zest, and preserved lemon with a pinch of sugar brings a tart, aromatic kick that makes it almost taste like candy, which explains why this is the only way my daughters will happily eat broccolini.

- ½ cup (120 g) olive oil
- 1 to 1½ tablespoons (20 to 30 g) seeded and finely chopped preserved lemons, homemade (page 41) or store-bought
- Grated zest of 2 lemons
- 2 tablespoons (30 g) fresh lemon juice
- ¼ teaspoon granulated sugar
- ½ teaspoon fine sea salt, or more to taste
- ½ teaspoon black pepper
- 1 pound (453 g) broccolini, tough ends trimmed
- ⅓ cup (40 g) panko breadcrumbs

1 Preheat the oven to 425°F (220°C) with the racks in the upper and lower thirds. Line one large and one small baking sheet with parchment paper.

2 Combine the olive oil, 1 tablespoon preserved lemon, the lemon zest, lemon juice, sugar, salt, and pepper in a medium bowl. Taste and adjust the seasoning, adding more salt and/or preserved lemon, ¼ teaspoon at a time, if desired.

3 Put the broccolini on the large baking sheet, drizzle about two-thirds of the marinade over it, and use your hands or tongs to toss to coat it, then spread it out in a single layer.

4 Toss the breadcrumbs with the remaining marinade in a small bowl until evenly moistened, then spread the crumbs out evenly on the small baking sheet.

5 Place both baking sheets in the oven, with the broccolini on the top rack and the breadcrumbs on the lower rack. Toast the breadcrumbs until golden brown, about 7 to 10 minutes; remove from the oven and set aside. Continue roasting the broccolini until it is tender and the tips are golden brown and crisp, about 10 to 15 minutes total.

6 Transfer the roasted broccolini to a large serving plate. Sprinkle the roasted breadcrumbs over the broccolini and serve.

roasted moroccan olives with feta

serves 4

Olives, a staple of the Moroccan table, as in other Mediterranean countries, are often generously set out in bowls with bread at the start of most meals. Moroccan olives can be prepared in various ways, but they are usually sold marinated with a burst of citrus and herbs or infused with a combination of warm spices, or sometimes both. Diced pickled vegetables such as carrots and chile peppers or chunks of preserved lemon can also be found in the mix. This is my go-to recipe when I am expecting guests and time is limited: fragrant, slightly lemony olives, with a hint of heat from harissa (if desired), paired with a block of baked feta drizzled with honey and good olive oil.

- ⅓ cup (80 g) olive oil, plus more for drizzling
- 1 cup (18 g) flat-leaf parsley leaves and tender stems, finely chopped
- 2 garlic cloves, minced or pressed
- 3 lemon slices, each cut into eighths, seeds removed
- 2 teaspoons harissa, homemade (page 44) or store-bought (optional)
- 1 teaspoon dried oregano
- 1 teaspoon sweet paprika
- 1 teaspoon ground cumin
- Pinch of fine sea salt
- 1¼ cups (175 g) drained pitted green, black, and/or purple olives
- One 7-ounce (198 g) block feta cheese
- 2 tablespoons (44 g) honey
- Bread or crackers for serving

1 Preheat the oven to 400°F (205°C). Combine the olive oil, parsley, garlic, lemon, harissa, if using, oregano, paprika, cumin, and salt in a large bowl and stir together. Add the olives and toss to coat with the marinade.

2 Choose a baking dish that is large enough to hold the feta with the olives arranged in around the cheese. Place the feta in the center of the dish, spoon the olives evenly around it, and pour the marinade remaining in the bowl over the feta and olives.

3 Transfer to the oven and bake for 25 minutes, or until the cheese is soft but not melted. Turn on the broiler and broil until the top of the cheese starts to brown and bubble, 2 to 3 minutes. (For those using a gas stove with a separate broiler drawer, they may need to adjust the rack position to ensure the feta is close to the heat source. Since broiler intensity can vary, I'd recommend keeping a close eye on it and adjusting the time as needed, maybe a bit longer if the heat isn't as direct as in an overhead broiler.)

4 Remove the baking dish from the oven, drizzle with the honey and olive oil. Serve immediately, with toasted baguette slices or crackers.

zucchini with parsley and garlicky warm croutons

serves 4

In this recipe, zucchini is prepared in a traditional Moroccan way, slowly simmered with a generous amount of olive oil and chopped tomatoes, flavored with garlic and spices. However, rather than simply serving it with bread on the side, I scatter freshly baked croutons, generously seasoned with more garlic and parsley, over the top of the cooked zucchini before serving. It's important to use warm, just-made croutons for this dish so they can absorb some of the fragrant zucchini juices while maintaining their satisfying crunch. I recommend a sourdough loaf for the croutons, but a classic French baguette or Italian ciabatta will also work. The zucchini can be served warm or at room temperature, making this a convenient dish for entertaining.

- ¼ cup (60 g) olive oil, plus more for drizzling
- 2 large zucchini (566 g), cut into slices ½ inch (1.2 cm) thick
- 2 medium tomatoes (200 g), halved and grated on the large holes of a box grater, or finely chopped, with their juices (alternatively, use half of a 14.5-ounce can of diced tomatoes)
- ¼ cup (24 g) flat-leaf parsley leaves and tender stems, finely chopped, plus more for garnish
- 4 garlic cloves, minced or pressed
- 2 teaspoons sweet paprika
- 1½ teaspoons ground cumin
- ¾ teaspoon fine sea salt, or more to taste, plus a large pinch
- ¼ teaspoon granulated sugar
- 2 cups (115 g) roughly torn pieces or 1-inch (2.5 cm) cubes of crusty white bread, such as sourdough (see headnote)

1 Preheat the oven to 400°F (205°C). Heat 2 tablespoons of the olive oil in a large frying pan over medium heat. Add the zucchini, tomatoes, 2 tablespoons of the parsley, half the garlic, the paprika, cumin, salt, and sugar, cover the pan, and cook over medium-low heat, stirring occasionally to keep the zucchini from sticking to the pan, for 15 to 18 minutes, or until the zucchini is soft.

2 Remove the lid, increase the heat to medium, and cook, stirring occasionally, until most of the liquid has evaporated, about 5 minutes. Taste and adjust the seasoning, adding more salt, if desired. Set aside until ready to serve. *(The zucchini can be prepared in advance and kept in a sealed container in the fridge for up to 3 days. Bring to room temperature or reheat gently before serving.)*

3 *While the zucchini is cooking, prepare the croutons*: Combine the remaining 2 tablespoons olive oil, garlic, and 2 tablespoons parsley, add a large pinch of salt, and stir to mix. Add the bread pieces and use your hands or a large spoon to toss the bread pieces with the olive oil and herb mixture to coat. Taste and add more salt if necessary.

4 Spread the bread pieces out in a single layer on a baking sheet lined with parchment paper. Transfer to the oven and bake for 10 to 12 minutes, until golden, flipping the bread pieces halfway through for even browning. Remove from the oven.

5 Scatter the warm croutons on top of the zucchini (I like to serve it directly from the pan while the zucchini is still warm), drizzle with olive oil, and serve immediately.

سلطة

VEGETARIAN

MEALS

charred cabbage with harissa and peanut butter sauce

serves 4 to 6

This recipe is another example of how a few humble ingredients can come together quickly to create a truly satisfying meal. But let's talk about cabbage. I've always enjoyed it in all the usual preparations, from slaws to stir-fries to hearty soups, but it wasn't until I tried a dish of roasted cabbage in a London restaurant that I realized that there is another way to cook and savor it. Something almost magical happens during the roasting process as the cabbage softens and begins to caramelize; it transforms its texture and flavors and turns into a delicious treat. Here the cabbage, accompanied by an easy harissa-and-peanut-butter sauce, inspired by the flavor profile often found in many Chinese and Thai dishes, takes center stage. The heat of the harissa beautifully complements the sweetness of the peanut butter and the charred cabbage.

- 2 small Napa cabbages (600 to 700g each) or 1 large green cabbage
- ⅓ cup plus 2 tablespoons (110 g) olive oil
- Fine sea salt
- ¼ cup (62 g) natural peanut butter
- 2 to 4 tablespoons (30 to 60 g) warm water
- 1½ tablespoons (33g) harissa, homemade (page 44) or store-bought, or more to taste
- 1½ teaspoons soy sauce, or more to taste
- Finely chopped chives for garnish

1 Preheat the oven to 425°F (220°C). Slice each cabbage lengthwise through the core into 4 wedges if using Napa cabbages, 8 wedges if using a green cabbage.

2 Transfer the cabbage to a baking sheet and drizzle ⅓ cup (80 g) olive oil over the wedges, using your hands or a brush to make sure that all sides of the wedges are coated with olive oil. Generously season the wedges with salt and arrange them cut side down on the baking sheet, leaving at least 1 inch (2.5 cm) of space between them; use two baking sheets if necessary to ensure that the cabbage will roast and char, not steam.

3 Roast the cabbage, flipping the wedges occasionally and rotating the positions of the pans halfway through if you are using two sheets, for 30 to 35 minutes if using Napa cabbage, 40 to 45 minutes if using green cabbage, until the wedges are soft and charred on top.

4 *Meanwhile, make the sauce*: Combine the peanut butter, 2 tablespoons warm water, the remaining 2 tablespoons olive oil, harissa, and soy sauce in a small bowl and stir until smooth. The sauce should be thick but pourable; adjust the consistency if necessary, adding up to 2 more tablespoons warm water, 1 tablespoon or so at a time. Taste and adjust the seasoning, adding more harissa and/or soy sauce if necessary. *(The sauce can be prepared up to 3 days in advance and kept in a sealed container in the fridge; bring to room temperature before using.)*

5 When the cabbage is ready, spread the sauce over the center of a large serving plate. Arrange the cabbage wedges on top of the sauce and garnish with the chives. Serve immediately.

ras el hanout mushroom tacos with tomato and cucumber salad

serves 4

One of my dreams is to explore Mexico and its cuisine and devour every taco variety imaginable there. Tacos are the perfect street food: handheld, bursting with flavor, and often spicy, they offer endless mouthwatering combinations of ingredients. While I daydream about my future taco adventures, I love experimenting with different ideas at home. This recipe is a Moroccan-inspired taco explosion. The hero here is the oyster mushroom: seasoned with ras el hanout and roasted until almost caramelized, it makes a deeply tasty and satisfying filling that might trick even an ardent meat lover. The classic Moroccan tomato and cucumber salad, which, curiously enough, is similar to pico de gallo, adds a burst of freshness, and the drizzle of green harissa oil brings a touch of heat, tying everything together.

- ⅓ cup (80 g) plus 2 tablespoons (30 g) olive oil
- 4 garlic cloves, minced or pressed
- 2 teaspoons ras el hanout, preferably homemade (page 38)
- 1¼ teaspoons fine sea salt
- ¼ teaspoon granulated sugar
- 1 pound (453 g) oyster mushrooms, sliced lengthwise into ¼-inch-thick (0.6 cm) strips
- ½ medium red onion (85 g), cut into ¼-inch-thick (0.6 cm) slices
- Eight 5-inch (12.7 cm) soft tortillas

tomato and cucumber salad

- 2 medium tomatoes (200 g), halved, seeded, and cut into ¼-inch (0.6 cm) dice
- Half a medium cucumber (150 g), peeled, halved lengthwise, seeded, and cut into ¼-inch (0.6 cm) dice
- Half a small yellow onion (60 g), finely chopped
- ½ cup flat-leaf parsley leaves and tender stems, finely chopped
- 1 tablespoon fresh lemon juice
- 1 tablespoon olive oil
- ¼ teaspoon fine sea salt, or more to taste
- Large pinch of black pepper

- 2 tablespoons (25 g) Green Harissa (page 47)
- 2 limes, halved
- Hot sauce for serving, such as Cholula (optional)

1 Preheat the oven to 400°F (205°C). Line a large baking sheet with parchment paper.

2 Combine the ⅓ cup (80 g) olive oil, garlic, ras el hanout, salt, and sugar in a small bowl and mix to combine. Put the mushrooms and onions on the lined pan, drizzle the olive oil mixture over them, and use your hands to coat them evenly, then spread them out on the baking sheet.

3 Transfer the pan to the oven and roast for 25 to 30 minutes, stirring halfway through, until the onions are soft and lightly browned and the mushrooms are tender, golden brown, and slightly charred in spots. Remove from the oven and set aside.

4 Meanwhile, combine the remaining 2 tablespoons (30 g) olive oil and the green harissa in a small bowl and stir until smooth. Cover and refrigerate until ready to use.

(recipe continues)

5 *Make the tomato and cucumber salad*: Combine the tomatoes, cucumber, onion, parsley, lemon juice, olive oil, salt, and pepper in a medium bowl and stir to mix. Taste and adjust the seasoning, adding more salt if necessary.

6 Warm 2 or 3 tortillas at a time (depending on the size of your pan) in a large frying pan over medium-high heat, turning once, for 15 to 20 seconds per side, until softened and pliable. Wrap them in a dish towel to keep warm until ready to serve. Alternatively, wrap the stack of tortillas in foil and heat them in a 300°F (150°C) oven for 10 minutes.

7 To assemble the tacos, divide the warm mushrooms among the tortillas and top with the tomato and cucumber salad. Drizzle the green harissa oil over the top and serve with the lime halves on the side to squeeze over the tacos. Serve with hot sauce on the side, if desired.

"bakoula" greens galette with burrata

serves 4

In Morocco and throughout the Maghreb, the term "kemia" refers to a selection of small dishes served at the beginning of a meal, similar to the mezze of other regions. These small dishes, which bring a variety of flavors, textures, and color to the meal, are usually categorized as raw or cooked salads. For instance, the Tomato and Cucumber Salad (page 122) and Green Pepper and Tomato Salsa (page 50) can both be served as part of a kemia spread; most vegetables can be turned into a kemia-style salad. Bakoula is a lemony, earthy, and fragrant cooked salad, traditionally prepared with mallow, a leafy green usually available during the warmer months between June and December. It's hard to source mallow outside Morocco, but Swiss chard and collard greens are good alternatives. For this galette, I use the cooked greens as the filling, enclosing them in buttery pastry and then topping the galette with creamy fresh burrata, for an unusual but very satisfying vegetarian meal.

crust

- 1¾ cups (210 g) all-purpose flour, plus more for rolling
- 1 teaspoon granulated sugar
- ½ teaspoon fine sea salt
- 8 tablespoons (113 g) cold unsalted butter
- 1 tablespoon fresh lemon juice
- 4 to 6 tablespoons (60 to 90 g) ice water

bakoula greens

- ¼ cup (60 g) olive oil, plus more for drizzling
- 2 pounds (906 g) Swiss chard or collard greens, thick stalks removed and cut crosswise into 3-inch-wide (7.6 cm) strips
- 1 cup (18 g) flat-leaf parsley leaves and tender stems, chopped
- 1 cup (18 g) cilantro leaves and tender stems, chopped
- 3 garlic cloves, minced or pressed
- 1½ teaspoons ground cumin
- 1¼ teaspoons sweet paprika
- ½ teaspoon fine sea salt, or more to taste
- 1 to 2 tablespoons (20 to 40 g) seeded and finely chopped preserved lemons, homemade (page 41) or store-bought
- 1½ tablespoons fresh lemon juice, or more to taste

- 1 egg, beaten
- 1 ball (4 to 6 ounces/113 to 170 g) burrata, drained, at room temperature
- Salt and black pepper, for seasoning

1 *Make the crust*: Mix together the flour, sugar, and salt in a large bowl. Using the large holes of a box grater, grate the cold butter into the bowl. (If you don't have a box grater, cut the butter into ½-inch/1.2 cm pieces and add to the bowl.) Use your fingertips to rub the butter into the flour until the mixture looks like breadcrumbs. Add the lemon juice and ¼ cup (60 g) ice water and use your hands to bring the dough together. If the dough is too dry, add up to 2 tablespoons (30 g) more water, ½ tablespoon at a time. Transfer the dough to a piece of parchment paper large enough to line a baking sheet, wrap it tightly, and refrigerate for 1 to 2 hours, until firm, or for up to 3 days. If you're in a hurry, you can chill the dough in the freezer for 20 to 30 minutes.

(recipe continues)

2 *Make the greens*: Heat the olive oil in a Dutch oven or other large heavy pot over medium-low heat. Add the Swiss chard or collard greens and toss to coat with the olive oil, then cover the pot and cook until the they are very soft, 8 to 10 minutes.

3 Uncover the pot and stir in the parsley, cilantro, garlic, cumin, paprika, and salt. Increase the heat to medium-high and cook, stirring frequently, until most of the liquid has evaporated, 8 to 10 minutes. Stir in 1 tablespoon of the preserved lemon and lemon juice, then taste and adjust the seasoning, adding more salt and/or more preserved lemon by the teaspoon, if desired. Remove the pot from the heat, transfer the greens to a bowl, and let cool. *(You can make the bakoula ahead and store in a sealed container in the fridge for up to 3 days.)*

4 *Assemble and bake the galette*: Preheat the oven to 400°F (205°C). Unwrap the dough and line a baking sheet with the parchment paper. On a floured surface, using a floured rolling pin, roll the dough out into a 14- to 15-inch (35 to 40 cm) round, starting from the center and rolling outward, and rotating the dough frequently. If necessary, trim the edges of the dough to even them. Lightly flour the dough, roll it up around the rolling pin, and carefully transfer to the lined baking sheet.

5 Spread the greens evenly over the dough, leaving a 2-inch (5 cm) border all around; reserve any juices left in the bowl. Fold the edges of the dough over the greens, pleating the dough as necessary, then press the pleats together to seal. Pour any reserved juices over the center of the greens, making sure to avoid the border of dough.

6 Brush the pastry with the beaten egg. Bake the galette for 40 to 45 minutes, or until the edges of the crust are golden brown.

7 Remove the galette from the oven. Place the burrata on top, cut it open, season with salt and pepper, drizzle with olive oil and serve immediately.

TIP: To save time, you can substitute store-bought puff pastry for the homemade dough.

eggplant tagine m'qualli

This is the eggplant version of one of the most popular Moroccan tagines, chicken with olives and preserved lemon (for an easy sheet-pan version of that recipe, see page 168). That tagine is often served with deep-fried eggplant slices. Inspired by this tradition, I created a version that celebrates the eggplant on its own, following the spirit of m'qualli tagines, with ground ginger, turmeric, and garlic in a fragrant, glossy onion sauce. I found that brushing the eggplant slices with oil and roasting them is a simpler way to achieve a similar texture to that of the traditional deep-fried version. This recipe is a lovely centerpiece for a special vegetarian dinner with friends, but I actually prepare it routinely, and I usually make double the amount to last throughout the week. Serve with bread, couscous, or rice.

- ⅔ cup (160 g) plus 3 tablespoons (45 g) olive oil
- 4 garlic cloves, minced or pressed
- Fine sea salt
- 1½ pounds (680 g) medium Italian eggplants (about 2 to 3), cut into ¾-inch-thick (1.9 cm) slices
- 2 large red onions (220 g), thinly sliced
- ¾ teaspoon ground turmeric
- ¾ teaspoon ground ginger
- Pinch of saffron threads (optional)
- 1 cup (18 g) cilantro leaves and tender stems, finely chopped, plus more for garnish
- ½ cup (120 g) vegetable stock or water, plus more if needed
- ¼ teaspoon black pepper
- ⅓ cup (46 g) pitted Kalamata olives or other brined olives, drained
- 2 to 3 teaspoons seeded and finely chopped preserved lemon, homemade (page 41) or store-bought

serves 4

1 Preheat the oven to 400°F (205°C) with the racks in the upper and lower thirds. Line two baking sheets with parchment paper.

2 Combine the ⅔ cup (160 g) olive oil, half the garlic, and ½ teaspoon salt in a liquid measuring cup or small bowl and stir to mix.

3 Cut the eggplants into ¾-inch-thick (1.9 cm) slices. Arrange the eggplant slices on the lined sheets and brush them on both sides with the olive oil mixture. Set aside.

4 Heat the remaining 3 tablespoons (45 g) olive oil in a large frying pan over medium-low heat. Add the onions, cover the pan, and cook, stirring occasionally, until the onions are soft and translucent, 10 to 12 minutes.

5 Add the remaining garlic, the turmeric, ginger, and saffron, if using, and cook, stirring occasionally, until fragrant, about 2 minutes. Add the cilantro, stock, ½ teaspoon salt, and the pepper and bring to a boil over high heat. Cover the pan, reduce the heat to low, and simmer for 45 to 50 minutes, until the sauce is glossy, has thickened, and its flavors have melded together. Stir the sauce every 15 to 20 minutes to prevent it from sticking to the bottom of the pan; if it looks like there isn't enough liquid in the pan at any point, add more stock or water 1 tablespoon at a time.

6 *Meanwhile, roast the eggplant*: As soon as the sauce starts simmering, transfer the eggplant to the oven and roast for 40 to 45 minutes, rotating the pans and switching racks halfway through, and flipping the eggplant slices for even browning, until soft and golden brown. Remove from the oven.

7 When the sauce is ready, stir in the olives and 2 teaspoons preserved lemon. Taste and adjust the seasoning, adding more salt and/or teaspoons of preserved lemon, if desired. Remove from the heat.

8 To serve, spread half of the onion sauce over the center of a large serving plate. Top with overlapping slices of the eggplant and spoon the remaining sauce over the eggplant. Garnish with finely chopped cilantro.

TIP: The onion sauce can be prepared up to 2 days in advance. Refrigerate in a sealed container and reheat in a large frying pan over medium-low heat before serving.

roasted spiced eggplant with yogurt and harissa chile crisp

serves 4 to 6

When I moved to London in 2010, I discovered a world where vegetables were not just sides but often the stars of the show. As I've always loved zaalouk, a Moroccan spiced eggplant and tomato dip (Eggplant Dip with Red Bell Pepper, page 106), I was excited to discover creative new ways to prepare eggplants. Here roasted eggplant is served with yogurt, a combination that has become a signature of Yotam Ottolenghi's cuisine, and drizzled with some of my Harissa Chile Crisp (page 47), adding fragrance, texture, and heat.

- 3 medium Italian eggplants or 3 small globe eggplants (906 g)
- ½ cup (120 g) olive oil
- 3 garlic cloves, minced or pressed
- 1¼ teaspoons sweet paprika
- 1¼ teaspoons ground cumin
- 1 teaspoon fine sea salt
- ¾ cup (180 g) Greek yogurt or whole-milk yogurt
- 1½ tablespoons (22 g) fresh lemon juice
- ¼ cup (52 g) Harissa Chile Crisp (page 47)
- Cilantro leaves for garnish

1 Preheat the oven to 400°F (205°C) with the racks in the upper and lower thirds. Line two baking sheets with parchment paper.

2 Use a vegetable peeler to peel strips of eggplant skin from the top to bottom of each eggplant, leaving alternating strips of white flesh. Cut the eggplants into ¾-inch-thick (1.9 cm) slices and arrange them on the lined sheets.

3 Combine the olive oil, garlic, paprika, cumin, and ¾ teaspoon of the salt in a small bowl and stir to mix. Drizzle the mixture evenly over the eggplant slices and use your hands to make sure the slices are well coated with the mixture.

4 Roast the eggplant, flipping the slices halfway through for even browning, for 40 to 45 minutes, until soft and golden brown. Remove from the oven and set aside to cool.

5 Combine the yogurt, lemon juice, and the remaining ¼ teaspoon salt in a small bowl and stir until smooth. If necessary, add a little water, 1 tablespoon at a time, until the yogurt reaches a pourable consistency.

6 To serve, arrange the eggplant slices, slightly overlapping, on a large serving platter. Spoon over the yogurt sauce and drizzle the chile crisp over the top. Garnish with cilantro leaves.

zaalouk and gruyère grilled cheese sandwiches

serves 4

Zaalouk, a favorite spiced eggplant dip (Eggplant Dip with Red Bell Pepper, page 106), has held a special place in my heart since I was a child. But there's another food that I've loved for as long as I can remember, and that is grilled cheese sandwiches. They were among the first things I ever made for myself growing up, though my sandwich-making skills have markedly evolved since those days. Here zaalouk elevates the flavor profile of this universally loved sandwich and gives it a touch of sophistication. Use good bread, such as a sourdough loaf, for these sandwiches; I prefer Gruyère cheese to the typical cheddar or American. Don't be tempted to increase the heat during the cooking process; keep the temperature low to allow the cheese to melt slowly and the bread to toast gradually for optimal results. My secret to the perfect grilled cheese is butter on the inside and mayonnaise on the outside. The butter delivers a classic, comforting flavor, while the mayonnaise ensures even browning and adds a delicate tang that beautifully compliments the cheese.

- 8 large slices bread, preferably sourdough
- ¼ cup (55 g) mayonnaise
- 4 tablespoons (60 g) unsalted butter, softened
- 1½ cups (385 g) Eggplant Dip with Red Bell Pepper–Zaalouk (page 106)
- 10 ounces (282 g) Gruyère cheese, shredded
- 1 to 2 tablespoons (15 to 30 g) olive oil

1 Lay 4 of the bread slices out on your work surface and spread about ½ tablespoon of mayonnaise over each slice. Flip the slices over and spread about ½ tablespoon butter on the other side of each slice. Spread 5 to 6 tablespoons zaalouk over each slice. Place a quarter of the Gruyère on top of the dip on each slice.

2 Lay the remaining 4 slices bread out on your worktop and spread about ½ tablespoon butter over each one. Place the slices butter side down on top of the Gruyère to make sandwiches and press down gently. Spread about ½ tablespoon of the remaining mayonnaise over the top of each sandwich.

3 Heat 1 tablespoon olive oil in a large cast-iron or other frying pan or griddle over medium-low heat. Add the sandwiches (cook them in two batches if necessary, using another tablespoon of oil if necessary), cover with a lid, and cook until the bottoms turn golden brown, 2 to 3 minutes. Use a spatula to flip the sandwiches, cover again, and cook until the bottoms are golden brown and the cheese has fully melted, 2 to 3 minutes.

4 Transfer the sandwiches to a plate, slice each one in half, and serve.

lentil stew with sun-dried tomatoes and kale—adis

serves 6

Adis is a traditional lentil stew made with just a few simple ingredients: lentils, onions, tomatoes, and spices. My mom used to prepare it for me when we lived in Brussels. (I was often anemic, and this dish has always been one of my favorite iron-rich meals.) Sometimes she would enhance it with some khlii (see Preserved Beef, page 73), or add leafy greens and carrots for a nutritional boost. In this version, I've opted for sun-dried tomatoes for their sweet, intense flavor and kale for its earthy notes as well as its nutritional value. The vinegary red onion topping is optional, but it brings an appealing sweet-tart punch to the dish. I usually serve this comforting stew with crusty bread, but rice and quinoa are also good options.

3 tablespoons (45 g) olive oil
1 large yellow onion (220 g), thinly sliced
3 garlic cloves, minced or pressed
2 teaspoons sweet paprika
½ teaspoon ground cumin
¼ teaspoon ground ginger
½ teaspoon ground turmeric
1 teaspoon fine sea salt, or more to taste
¼ teaspoon black pepper
1½ cups (315 g) dried brown lentils, rinsed and drained
3 medium tomatoes (300 g), halved and grated on the large holes of a box grater, or finely chopped, with their juices (alternatively, use two-thirds of a 14.5-ounce can of diced tomatoes)
½ cup (80 g) oil-packed sun-dried tomatoes, drained and sliced into ¼-inch-wide (0.6 cm) strips
1 cup (18 g) cilantro leaves and tender stems, finely chopped, plus more for garnish
4½ cups (1080 g) vegetable stock or water, plus more if needed
2 cups (80 g) chopped kale (thick stalks removed)

vinegary red onion topping (optional)

1 small red onion (120 g), finely chopped
2½ tablespoons (40 g) white wine vinegar
¼ teaspoon granulated sugar
Pinch of fine sea salt

1 Heat the olive oil in a large pot over medium-low heat. Add the onions, cover the pot, and cook, stirring occasionally, until soft and translucent, 10 to 12 minutes.

2 Add the garlic, paprika, cumin, ginger, turmeric, salt, and pepper and cook, stirring occasionally, until fragrant, about 3 minutes. Add the lentils, tomatoes, sun-dried tomatoes, cilantro, and stock or water and bring to a boil over high heat. Reduce the heat to low, cover the pot, and simmer for 30 to 40 minutes, until the lentils are nearly tender but still hold their shape. Stir occasionally to prevent them from sticking, and add more stock or water as needed if the stew becomes too thick.

3 *Meanwhile, if desired, make the vinegary red onion topping*: Combine the chopped red onion, vinegar, sugar, and salt in a small bowl and let stand for at least 10 minutes.

4 When the lentils are nearly ready, stir in the kale and cook until it is wilted and tender and the lentils are soft, 5 to 7 minutes. Taste and adjust the seasoning, adding more salt if necessary.

5 Ladle the lentil stew into shallow bowls, top with the vinegary onion topping, if you made it, and serve immediately.

berber vegetarian skillet tagine with olive, preserved lemon, and cilantro salsa

serves 4

Anyone who is at all familiar with Moroccan cuisine knows about tagines: meat or chicken and/or vegetables bathed in a seasoning mixture made with spices and cooked slowly until fork-tender and succulent. This recipe opts for using a covered heavy skillet in the oven instead of the classic clay pot over charcoal. While this method deviates from tradition, the end result has all the flavors and textures of a traditional tagine. The olive, preserved lemon, and cilantro salsa adds a salty, briny punch that brings brightness, color, and texture to the dish. To achieve a symmetrical presentation of the tagine, aim to cut the vegetables into similar lengths.

- ¼ cup (60 g) vegetable stock or water
- 2 tablespoons (30 g) olive oil
- 3 garlic cloves, minced or pressed
- 1 teaspoon ground turmeric
- 1 teaspoon sweet paprika
- 1 teaspoon ground ginger
- ½ teaspoon ground cumin
- 1¼ teaspoons fine sea salt
- ¼ teaspoon black pepper
- 1 large yellow onion (220 g), sliced
- 1 large Yukon Gold potato (300 g), peeled and cut into ¾-inch-thick (1.9 cm) wedges
- 2 large carrots (160 g), halved crosswise and cut lengthwise into quarters
- 1 medium red bell pepper (140 g), cored, seeded, and sliced lengthwise into ¾-inch-wide (1.9 cm) strips
- 1 large zucchini (300 g), halved crosswise and cut lengthwise into quarters
- 1 cup cherry tomatoes (150 g), halved lengthwise
- ½ cup Olive, Preserved Lemon, and Cilantro Salsa (page 49)
- Bread for serving

1 Preheat the oven to 350°F (175°C).

2 Combine the stock or water, olive oil, garlic, turmeric, paprika, ginger, cumin, salt, and pepper in a small bowl. Set aside.

3 Grab a large, deep, ovenproof frying pan, ideally a heavy-bottomed 10-inch (25 cm) pan with a lid, such as a cast-iron skillet. Spread the onions over the bottom of the pan. Mound the potato wedges in the center of the pan. Arrange the carrots around the potatoes, leaning them against the potatoes. Alternate the bell pepper strips and zucchini around the carrots, leaning them against the carrots. Scatter the cherry tomatoes around the vegetables. Pour the stock mixture over the vegetables and cover the pan tightly with a lid (or a double layer of foil, preferably heavy-duty).

4 Transfer the pan to the oven and cook for 60 to 70 minutes, or until the potato wedges are tender.

5 Remove the pan from the oven, uncover it, and spoon the salsa over the tagine. Serve immediately, with bread on the side.

artichoke and pea tagine pasta

serves 4 to 6

This is my take on a traditional artichoke and pea tagine, a popular dish typically enjoyed during springtime. In Moroccan homes, tagines are served simply with bread, without sides like rice or pasta. But I have found that some of our tagines make excellent sauces for pasta. Here, the artichokes and peas are seasoned the traditional m'qualli way, with garlic, ground ginger, and turmeric. The dish is finished with preserved lemon and olives, common ingredients in this tagine, which add a light, briny touch. The canned artichoke hearts, frozen peas, and olives ensure you can enjoy this wholesome meal year-round, regardless of the season.

- ⅓ cup (80 g) olive oil, plus more for serving
- 1 large onion (220 g), thinly sliced
- 5 garlic cloves, minced or pressed
- 1½ teaspoons ground turmeric
- 1½ teaspoons ground ginger
- 1¼ cups (300 g) vegetable stock
- 2 cups (36 g) flat-leaf parsley leaves and tender stems, finely chopped
- 2 teaspoons fine sea salt, more to taste
- ¼ teaspoon freshly ground black pepper
- Generous pinch of granulated sugar
- 12 ounces (340 g) spaghetti or other dried pasta of your choice
- Two 14-ounce (400 g) cans artichoke hearts, drained and quartered lengthwise
- 1 cup (170 g) frozen peas
- 1 cup (140 g) pitted Kalamata olives or other red-brown olives, drained and quartered lengthwise
- 1 to 2 tablespoons (20 to 40 g) seeded, and finely chopped preserved lemons, homemade (page 41) or store-bought
- ¼ cup (30 g) finely grated Parmesan for serving

1 Heat the olive oil in a large frying pan over medium heat. Add the onions, garlic, turmeric, and ginger and cook, stirring frequently, until fragrant, 3 to 4 minutes.

2 Add the stock, parsley, 1 teaspoon of the salt, the pepper and sugar, and bring to a boil over high heat, scraping the bottom of the pan occasionally. Cover the pan, reduce the heat to low, and simmer, stirring occasionally so the onions don't stick to the bottom of the pan, for 35 minutes, or until the onions are soft, translucent, and infused with the color and flavors of the spices.

3 Meanwhile, set a large pot of water over high heat, add the remaining teaspoon of salt, and bring to a boil. About 10 minutes before the sauce is ready, add the pasta to the boiling water and cook according to the package instructions until it's almost al dente. Reserve 1 cup of the cooking water and drain the pasta.

4 About 5 minutes before the pasta is done, remove the lid from the pan containing the sauce, increase the heat to medium-low, and add the artichokes, peas, olives, and 1 tablespoon preserved lemon. Cook, stirring frequently, until the peas are tender and the artichokes are warmed through.

5 Return the drained pasta to the pot, add the sauce, and stir well to combine. Cook over low heat, stirring occasionally and adding some of the reserved cooking water, 1 tablespoon at a time if necessary to loosen the sauce. Taste and adjust the seasoning with more salt and/or teaspoons of the preserved lemon if desired.

6 Serve immediately, topped with a generous drizzle of olive oil and the grated Parmesan.

harira

serves 6

There are many soups in Moroccan cuisine, but if there is just one that best represents our culture, it is harira. The word "harira" is derived from the Arabic word "harir," which means "silk" and refers to the soup's appealingly silky texture. Traditionally made with a broth flavored with aromatic spices such as cinnamon, ginger, and turmeric, along with cilantro, harira gains its distinctive consistency from the tedwira, a thickening agent made with flour and water. The word "tedwira" means "stirring" in Moroccan Arabic, and the name refers to the act of stirring that liquid as it's added to the pot toward the end of the cooking process.

Although it is enjoyed throughout the year, harira is especially meaningful to many Moroccans during Ramadan. It's commonly served to break the fast, and for many, its absence at the break-fast table can feel like a missing piece.

- 3 tablespoons (45 g) olive oil
- 1 medium onion (170 g), finely diced
- 3 celery stalks (195 g), minced or finely chopped
- 2 teaspoons ground turmeric
- 2 teaspoons ground ginger
- ¼ cup (60 g) tomato paste
- 8 medium tomatoes (800 g), halved and grated on the large holes of a box grater, or finely chopped, with their juices (alternatively, use two 14.5-ounce cans of diced tomatoes)
- 1 cup (18 g) flat-leaf parsley leaves and tender stems, finely chopped
- 8 cups (1920 g) vegetable stock or water
- 1 tablespoon fine sea salt, or more to taste
- ¾ teaspoon black pepper
- One 15-ounce (425 g) can chickpeas, drained and rinsed
- One 15-ounce (425 g) can lentils, drained and rinsed
- 2 cups (36 g) cilantro leaves and tender stems, finely chopped, plus more for garnish
- 2 ounces (56 g) spaghetti, broken into 1-inch (2.5 cm) pieces, or broken vermicelli
- 3 tablespoons (22 g) all-purpose flour
- ⅓ cup (80 g) warm water

1 Heat the olive oil in a large pot over medium-low heat. Add the onions and celery, cover the pot, and cook, stirring occasionally, until the vegetables are soft and translucent, about 7 minutes.

2 Add the turmeric, ginger, and tomato paste and cook, stirring occasionally, until fragrant, about 2 minutes. Add the tomatoes, lentils, cilantro, parsley, stock or water, salt, and pepper and bring to a boil over high heat. Cover the pot, reduce the heat to low, and simmer for 50 to 60 minutes, or until the flavors of the soup have melded together and the color is no longer bright red.

3 Meanwhile, combine the flour and warm water in a small bowl and stir until well blended and there are no lumps. Set aside.

4 Add the chickpeas and lentils to the pot and bring to a simmer. Slowly add the flour and water mixture, stirring constantly for a minute or two to distribute the mixture evenly in the soup, preventing it from clumping or sticking to the bottom of the pot. Bring to a simmer and simmer for 7 to 10 minutes until the soup has thickened slightly.

5 Add the cilantro and spaghetti or vermicelli, bring back to a simmer, and cook until the spaghetti or vermicelli is just al dente, about 5 to 7 minutes (or according to the package instructions). Turn off the heat immediately, as the pasta will continue cooking with the residual heat. If too much liquid has evaporated during cooking, add more water as necessary to achieve the desired consistency. Taste and adjust the seasoning with more salt if necessary.

6 Ladle the soup into bowls, garnish generously with chopped cilantro, and serve with lemon wedges on the side.

creamy preserved-lemon tomato soup

serves 6

The combination of tomatoes and preserved lemons might seem unusual but their flavors harmonize beautifully in this bright, comforting soup. Although both preserved lemons and tomatoes are acidic, the heavy cream mellows that sharpness and brings out the sweetness of the tomatoes and aromas of the preserved lemons. The result is a cozy soup that is welcome once cold nights set in. I like to serve it with my Zaalouk and Gruyère Grilled Cheese Sandwiches (page 132) for a Moroccan variation on that popular combination.

- 3 tablespoons (45 g) olive oil, plus more for drizzling
- 2 large onions (440 g), thinly sliced
- 4 garlic cloves, minced or pressed
- 1½ tablespoons dried oregano
- 1½ teaspoons fine sea salt, or more to taste
- ¾ teaspoon black pepper, or more to taste
- Two 28-ounce (795 g) cans crushed tomatoes, preferably San Marzano, with their juices
- 2 cups (480 g) vegetable stock or water
- 2½ tablespoons (55 g) honey, or more to taste
- ¾ cup (180 g) heavy cream, plus more for drizzling
- 1½ to 3 tablespoons (30 to 60 g) seeded and finely chopped preserved lemons, homemade (page 41) or store-bought

1 Heat the olive oil in a large pot over medium-low heat. Add the onions, cover the pot, and cook, stirring occasionally, until the onions are soft and translucent, 10 to 12 minutes.

2 Add the garlic, oregano, salt, and pepper and cook, stirring occasionally, until fragrant, about 2 minutes. Add the crushed tomatoes, with their juices, the stock or water, and honey and bring to a boil over high heat. Cover the pot, reduce the heat to low, and simmer for 1 hour to meld the flavors and create a richer, more flavorful base for the soup.

3 Add the cream and 1½ tablespoons preserved lemon to the soup and use an immersion blender to blend until smooth. Alternatively, allow the soup to cool slightly (to avoid burning yourself with the steam) and, working in batches, blend in a stand blender, return to the pot, and reheat gently if necessary.

4 Taste the soup and adjust the seasoning, adding more salt, pepper, honey, and/or preserved lemon if necessary. Ladle the soup into bowls and garnish with a drizzle of heavy cream, another of olive oil, and a sprinkle of oregano.

egg and tomato tagine with tangy cilantro oil

serves 4

Many people know this dish as "shakshuka," but in Morocco, it's "tagine dial beid wa maticha," or egg-and-tomato tagine. The original dish came from Tunisia, where the tomato sauce usually includes bell peppers and chiles. The concept of eggs cooked in tomato sauce is part of many different cuisines: as eggs in purgatory in Italy, for example, or menemen in Turkey. The Italian version typically consists of eggs poached in a spicy tomato sauce. In Turkey, eggs are scrambled with tomatoes, peppers, onions, and spices to make menemen. I've been refining my egg-and-tomato tagine recipe for years, and I've discovered that a drizzle of homemade cilantro oil really brings out all the flavors, and brightens this classic dish.

- 2 tablespoons (30 g) olive oil
- 1 medium onion (170 g), grated or finely chopped
- 2 garlic cloves, minced or pressed
- 1½ teaspoons sweet paprika
- 1 teaspoon ground cumin
- One 14-ounce (396 g) can crushed tomatoes
- 1 cup (18 g) flat-leaf parsley leaves and tender stems, finely chopped
- ½ teaspoon granulated sugar
- ½ teaspoon fine sea salt, or more to taste
- ¼ teaspoon black pepper

cilantro oil

- ¼ cup (60 g) olive oil
- 1½ cups (27 g) cilantro leaves and tender stems
- 2 teaspoons white wine vinegar
- ½ teaspoon fine sea salt, or more to taste
- ¼ teaspoon granulated sugar, or more to taste

- 4 large eggs
- Bread for serving

1 Heat the olive oil in a large frying pan over medium-low heat. Add the onion, garlic, paprika, and cumin and cook, stirring occasionally, until fragrant, 1 to 2 minutes. Add the crushed tomatoes, parsley, sugar, salt, and pepper, increase the heat to medium-high, and bring to a boil. Cover the pan, reduce the heat to low, and simmer for 35 to 40 minutes, stirring every 10 to 15 minutes to prevent sticking, until the tomatoes have reduced to a fragrant, velvety sauce. If it looks as if the sauce is too dry at any point, add 1 to 2 tablespoons of water.

2 *Meanwhile, make the cilantro oil*: Combine the olive oil, cilantro, vinegar, salt, and sugar in a food processor and process until the cilantro is finely chopped. (If you don't have a food processor, chop the cilantro as fine as you can with a sharp knife and then combine with the rest of the ingredients.) Taste and adjust the seasoning, adding more salt or sugar if necessary. Set aside. *(You can make the oil ahead and store it in a sealed container in the fridge for up to 2 days. Bring to room temperature before using.)*

3 Taste the tomato sauce and adjust the seasoning, adding more salt if necessary. Use the back of a large spoon to make 4 wells in the sauce, then gently crack an egg into each well. Cover the pan and cook for 5 to 6 minutes, until the whites are set but the yolks are still runny.

4 Drizzle the cilantro oil over the eggs and tomato sauce and serve immediately, with bread on the side.

ⴰⴼⵓⵍⵍⵓⵙ
دجاج

CHICKEN

AQUAFINA

chicken and lentils in onion sauce with pasta–pappardelle r'fissa

serves 4 to 6

This recipe is a modern take on the centuries-old celebratory Moroccan dish r'fissa. Originating in the Fez region, r'fissa, a stew of braised chicken and lentils cooked in a fragrant onion sauce, is traditionally served with a thin dough known as "trid," cut into long strips. Trid has a texture similar to phyllo dough, but it is steamed rather than baked or fried, which makes it soft and pliable, like very thin crêpes. Over time, it has become common in Morocco to use different types of bread for r'fissa. The most common substitute is plain m'semen (see Garlic Butter and Cheese Flatbreads, page 75), cut into strips, but some cooks use other breads, like batbout (see 20-Minute Panfried Bread, page 86) or harcha (see Semolina Bread, page 60). I like to use pappardelle; although it is certainly not Moroccan, the texture and shape of these noodles surprisingly resembles trid strips, making them a practical substitute. For this dish, the chicken, lentils, and onions are simmered in a broth infused with ras el hanout, saffron, and herbs until the broth thickens and transforms into a glossy onion sauce for serving over the trid, or pappardelle.

- 5 tablespoons (75 g) olive oil
- 2½ pounds (1133 g) bone-in, skin-on chicken thighs (about 6 thighs)
- 3 large onions (660 g), thinly sliced
- 4 garlic cloves, minced or pressed
- Pinch of saffron threads (3 or 4 threads)
- 1 teaspoon ground turmeric
- 1 teaspoon ground ginger
- 1 teaspoon ras el hanout, preferably homemade (page 38)
- Fine sea salt
- ½ teaspoon black pepper, plus more to serve, if desired
- 2 cups (480 g) vegetable stock or water, plus more if needed
- ⅔ cup (140 g) dried brown lentils, rinsed and drained
- 1 cup (18 g) cilantro leaves and tender stems, finely chopped, plus more for garnish
- 1 pound (453 g) pappardelle or tagliatelle
- 2 tablespoons toasted sliced almonds (optional)

1 Heat 3 tablespoons (45 g) of the olive oil in a Dutch oven or other large heavy pot over medium-high heat. Pat the chicken thighs dry with paper towels. Working in batches of 3 thighs each, add the chicken skin-side-down to the hot oil; you should hear a distinct sizzle. Cook until the skin is golden brown and releases easily from the pot with a gentle lift using tongs, 5 to 7 minutes. Transfer the seared chicken (cooked only on the skin side) to a plate and set aside.

(recipe continues)

2 Reduce the heat to medium-low, add the onions to the pot, cover, and cook, stirring occasionally, until the onions are soft and translucent, about 10 minutes. Add the garlic, saffron, turmeric, ginger, ras el hanout, 1 teaspoon salt, and the pepper and cook, stirring frequently, until the mixture is fragrant, about 3 minutes.

3 Return the chicken thighs to the pot, add the stock or water, lentils, and cilantro, and bring to a boil over high heat. Reduce the heat to low, cover the pot, and cook, stirring occasionally, until the chicken is cooked through, 40 to 45 minutes.

4 Check the consistency of the sauce; it should be smooth and glossy and coat the back of a spoon. If it seems dry or too thick, add a few tablespoons of stock or water and stir to incorporate. Or, if the sauce is too thin, transfer the chicken thighs to a plate and continue simmering the sauce, uncovered, to thicken it slightly. This process may take a few minutes, so keep an eye on the sauce and stir occasionally to prevent sticking, then return the chicken to the pot. Taste the sauce and adjust the seasoning with salt if necessary.

5 Meanwhile, about 15 to 20 minutes before the chicken is cooked and the sauce is ready, set a large pot of water over high heat, add 1 teaspoon salt, and bring to a boil. Add the pappardelle and cook according to the package instructions; drain. Transfer the pasta to a large bowl, add the remaining 2 tablespoons olive oil, and toss the pasta to coat.

6 Divide the pappardelle among shallow serving plates and top with the chicken and plenty of the sauce. Garnish with chopped cilantro, the almonds, and black pepper, if desired, and serve.

quick chicken bastilla puff pies

makes 6 puff pies

Chicken bastilla is known to any Moroccan food aficionado as the cuisine's most iconic and decadent dish. It is a sweet-and-savory pie, traditionally made with layers of cooked chicken, caramelized onions, roasted almonds, and scrambled eggs enclosed in warqa, a pastry dough that is similar to phyllo. Preparing it is usually a labor-intensive, somewhat demanding affair, but my quick version delivers the authentic flavors without the hassle. These individual pies are made with store-bought puff pastry, and the filling can be prepared up to 2 days ahead. They are elegant enough for a special gathering but simple enough to put together for a weeknight dinner.

- 1 cup (100 g) sliced almonds
- ¼ cup (60 g) olive oil
- 1 pound (453 g) yellow onions (2 large or 3 medium), thinly sliced
- 2 tablespoons (44 g) honey, or more to taste
- 3 tablespoons (18 g) finely chopped cilantro leaves and tender stems
- 2 garlic cloves, minced or pressed
- 1 teaspoon ground turmeric
- 1 teaspoon ground ginger
- Heaping ½ teaspoon ground cinnamon
- Fine sea salt
- 3 large eggs, beaten with a fork
- 1¼ cups (200 g) cooked chicken in bite-size chunks
- 2 sheets puff pastry, such as Dufour (about 14 ounces/390 g each)
- All-purpose flour for rolling

cinnamon sugar (optional)

- 1 teaspoon confectioners' sugar
- ¼ teaspoon ground cinnamon

1 Preheat the oven to 350°F (175°C). Spread the sliced almonds evenly in a single layer on a baking sheet and toast in the oven for 7 to 10 minutes, until golden. Remove from the oven and set aside.

2 Meanwhile, heat 3 tablespoons (45 g) of the olive oil in a large frying pan over low heat. Add the onions, cover, and cook, stirring occasionally, until the onions are soft and translucent, about 15 minutes.

3 Add the honey, cilantro, garlic, turmeric, ginger, cinnamon, and 1 teaspoon salt to the pan and cook uncovered, stirring occasionally, for 10 minutes, or until the onions start to caramelize and there's no longer any liquid left (from cooking the onions) in the bottom of the pan. Remove from the heat and set aside.

(recipe continues)

4 *While the onions are caramelizing, cook the eggs*: Transfer about 2 tablespoons of the beaten eggs to a small bowl and set aside. Heat the remaining 1 tablespoon olive oil in a small frying pan over medium heat. Add the remaining eggs and a pinch of salt and cook, stirring gently with a wooden spoon, until the scrambled eggs are fully set, just a few minutes.

5 Add the scrambled eggs to the caramelized onions, along with the chicken and toasted almonds, and stir to combine. Taste the filling and add more salt and/or honey if necessary; set aside to cool. *(The filling can be prepared up to 2 days ahead and kept in a sealed container in the fridge.)*

6 Preheat the oven to 400°F (205°C). Line a baking sheet with parchment paper.

7 Unfold the puff pastry sheets onto a lightly floured surface. Run a rolling pin over the pastry sheets to eliminate any folds. Cut each sheet into 6 equal dough rectangles (or squares).

8 Divide the filling mixture evenly among 6 of the dough rectangles (about ½ cup each), leaving a border of about ½ inch (1.2 cm) all around the filling. Place a second dough rectangle on top of each filled rectangle and crimp the edges with a fork to seal. Brush the pies with the reserved beaten egg. *(You can assemble the pies up to 2 days ahead and keep them in a sealed container in the fridge.)*

9 Transfer the pies to the prepared baking sheet and bake for 20 to 25 minutes, until golden brown. Remove from the oven, dust with the cinnamon sugar, if desired, and serve.

sticky orange and turmeric chicken skewers

serves 4

This easy recipe is in no way traditional, but for me it epitomizes the ingredients and aromas of a flavor-packed journey through Morocco: the aroma of orange zest, the kick of turmeric, and the earthy notes of dried mint, brought together with a drizzle of honey. I prefer thighs when it comes to chicken skewers, but you can use boneless breasts if you like. This is a great appetizer, but it also makes a nice main course for 2 people.

Orange and Turmeric Marinade (page 43)

1 pound (450 g) skinless, boneless chicken thighs or breasts, cut into bite-size (1-inch/2.5 cm) chunks

1 tablespoon honey, or more to taste

Fine sea salt if needed

Cooked couscous and tomato salad to serve (optional)

1 Transfer half the marinade to a large container or bowl, add the chicken, and stir to coat. Cover and set aside for 15 minutes, or refrigerate for up to 24 hours. Cover the remaining marinade and refrigerate.

2 If using bamboo skewers, soak them in water to cover for 30 minutes; drain.

3 When ready to serve, thread the chicken pieces onto skewers. Transfer the remaining marinade to a small saucepan, add the honey, and simmer over medium-low heat, stirring frequently, until it has reduced to a sticky glaze, 8 to 10 minutes. Taste and adjust the seasoning, adding more salt and/or honey if necessary; remove from the heat and cover to keep warm.

4 Meanwhile, prepare a medium-hot fire in a charcoal or gas grill, or preheat a griddle pan over medium-high heat.

5 Arrange the skewers on the grill or in the griddle pan and cook, turning a couple of times, until cooked through, 3 to 4 minutes per side.

6 Transfer the skewers to a platter or individual plates, brush with the glaze, and serve immediately with couscous and tomato salad, if desired.

oven-baked cornflake-crusted chicken tenders with sweet chermoula sauce

serves 6

Growing up, when we went out for dinner, my brothers and I each had our favorite items on the kids' menu. For me, it was always chicken tenders, no matter the occasion. There's something undeniably satisfying about chicken fingers coated in a crispy crust, especially when dipped into a flavorful sauce. This version maintains the spirit of classic chicken tenders, but with a Moroccan twist. I added spices to the batter for the chicken for more flavor and used ground cornflakes for the crispy coating. The toasted corn flavor and subtle sweetness of the crumbs makes the chicken tenders special, but the real star is the Sweet Chermoula (page 42); cooking it until it thickens transforms it into a delicious dipping sauce.

- ¾ cup (235 g) Sweet Chermoula (page 42)
- 5 cups (140 g) cornflakes
- 1 large egg
- 2 tablespoons (27 g) mayonnaise
- 2 tablespoons (15 g) all-purpose flour
- 2 teaspoons sweet smoked paprika
- 2 teaspoons ground cumin
- 1 teaspoon garlic powder
- 1 teaspoon fine sea salt
- ½ teaspoon black pepper
- 1¼ pounds (567 g) chicken tenders, or chicken breasts cut into 1½-inch-long (3.7 cm) strips
- ¼ cup (60 g) olive oil
- Flaky salt, such as Maldon, to serve (optional)

1 Pour the chermoula into a small saucepan, bring to a simmer, and simmer over medium-low heat, stirring frequently, until it thickens slightly, reduces by about a third, and becomes glossy, 8 to 10 minutes.

2 Remove the sauce from the heat and let cool (the sauce will continue to thicken as it cools). Then cover and set aside until ready to serve. *(The sauce can be prepared up to 3 days in advance and refrigerated in a sealable container; reheat gently over low heat before serving.)*

3 Preheat the oven to 400°F (205°C). Line a baking sheet with parchment paper.

4 Put the cornflakes in a food processor and pulse until coarsely ground. Alternatively, place the cornflakes in a resealable plastic bag and crush with a rolling pin. Transfer the ground cornflakes to a shallow bowl or pie plate.

5 Combine the egg, mayonnaise, flour, smoked paprika, cumin, garlic powder, salt, and pepper in a large bowl and whisk until smooth. Working in batches, add the chicken pieces to the batter and turn to coat, then coat in the cornflakes, pressing gently on both sides so the crumbs adhere to the chicken, and place on the prepared baking sheet, leaving space between the pieces.

6 Drizzle the olive oil evenly over the chicken and bake for 15 to 20 minutes, depending on the thickness of the chicken, until it is cooked through and the coating is golden brown and crispy.

7 Remove from the oven, finish with flaky salt if using, and serve with the sauce.

chicken tagine à l'orange

serves 4

Not many tagines use fruits as the centerpiece; this one celebrates the orange, one of Morocco's most treasured fruits. If you visit Morocco, you will see orange trees lining our streets and dozens of carts selling freshly squeezed orange juice scattered throughout the alleys of the souks. Moroccan oranges are unlike any other: sweet and intensely flavorful, with hints of peach, and subtly tangy. What I love most about this sweet and savory tagine is that oranges are used in three different ways: the zest and juice add vibrancy to the onion braising sauce, and orange slices, cooked until soft and lightly caramelized, are served on top of the crispy chicken to be eaten whole. The result is a unique, truly delectable dish.

- 3 tablespoons (45 g) olive oil
- 2½ pounds (1133 g) bone-in, skin-on chicken thighs (6 to 8 thighs)
- Fine sea salt
- 2 yellow onions (340 g), finely chopped
- 3 garlic cloves, minced or pressed
- ¾ teaspoon ground turmeric
- ¾ teaspoon ground ginger
- ¾ teaspoon ground coriander
- ¼ teaspoon black pepper
- 1 teaspoon grated orange zest
- ¼ cup (60 g) fresh orange juice (from 1 large orange)
- ¼ cup (60 g) vegetable stock or water
- 1 cup (18 g) cilantro leaves and tender stems, finely chopped

caramelized orange slices

- 1 large orange (220 g), cut into ¼-inch-thick (0.6 cm) slices (including peel)
- ⅓ cup (80 g) water
- ⅓ cup (66 g) granulated sugar
- 1½ tablespoons (33 g) honey
- ⅛ teaspoon fine sea salt
- ⅛ teaspoon ground cinnamon

Toasted sesame seeds for garnish (optional)

1 Preheat the oven to 350°F (175°C). Heat the olive oil in a large, deep, ovenproof frying pan, ideally a heavy-bottomed 10-inch (25 cm) pan, over medium-high heat.

2 Meanwhile, pat the chicken thighs dry with paper towels. Season the chicken on both sides with ½ teaspoon salt. Working in batches of 3 to avoid crowding the pan, add the chicken thighs skin side down to the hot oil; you should hear a distinct sizzle. Cook until the skin is golden brown and releases easily from the pan with a gentle lift using tongs, 5 to 7 minutes. Transfer the seared chicken (cooked only on the skin side) to a plate and set aside.

3 Reduce the heat under the pan to medium-low and add the onions. Cover the pan and cook, stirring occasionally and scraping the bottom of the pan to prevent sticking, until the onions are soft and translucent, about 10 minutes. Add the garlic, turmeric, ginger, coriander, ¾ teaspoon salt, and the pepper and cook, stirring frequently, until fragrant, about 3 minutes.

(recipe continues)

4 Add the orange zest and juice, stock or water, and cilantro to the pan and stir to combine. Return the chicken thighs to the pan, skin side up, and bring the stock to a boil over high heat.

5 Transfer the pan to the oven and cook, uncovered, for 40 to 45 minutes, or until the chicken is golden and cooked through; check the pan every 15 minutes or so to make sure the liquid hasn't evaporated, and, if necessary, add more stock or water. Remove the chicken from the oven.

6 *Meanwhile, prepare the caramelized orange slices*: Put the orange slices in a medium heatproof bowl, cover them with boiling water, and let sit for 90 seconds. Drain immediately and pat dry with a kitchen towel.

7 Combine the water, sugar, honey, salt, and cinnamon in a small (8-inch/20 cm) frying pan and bring to a boil over medium-high heat, stirring until the sugar dissolves. Add the orange slices, reduce the heat to medium-low, and simmer, flipping the oranges occasionally, until the rinds soften and the sauce thickens to a thin, runny caramel, 20 to 25 minutes. Turn off the heat and cover the oranges to keep warm until ready to serve. (If necessary, reheat the orange slices over low heat before serving.)

8 Arrange the orange slices over the chicken, drizzle the caramel orange sauce over the top, sprinkle with sesame seeds, if using, and serve.

fragrant chicken and onions buried in couscous–seffa medfouna

serves 6

"Medfouna" means "buried" in Moroccan Arabic and it refers to the chicken and spiced braised onions that are hidden between layers of couscous. The first time I tried seffa was at a family party when I was just seven years old, where I noticed an impressive dome of couscous, garnished with dried fruits and almonds. When my mother served me a bowl, the blend of fragrant chicken, fluffy couscous, sweet raisins, and crunchy almonds was irresistible, and it instantly became one of my favorite dishes. If you like, you can substitute vermicelli for the couscous, keeping in mind that for this particular dish, vermicelli is steamed and, as a result, will take longer to cook.

- 1 cup (100 g) sliced almonds
- 3 tablespoons (45 g) olive oil
- 1 tablespoon ghee (see Tip) or unsalted butter
- 4 large yellow onions (880 g), thinly sliced
- 4 garlic cloves, minced or pressed
- Generous pinch of saffron threads
- 1½ teaspoons ground turmeric
- 1½ teaspoons ground ginger
- ½ teaspoon ground cinnamon
- 1½ teaspoons fine sea salt, or more to taste
- ½ teaspoon black pepper
- 2½ pounds (1132 g) boneless, skinless chicken breasts or thighs, cut lengthwise into strips 1½ inches (3.8 cm) thick
- 1 cup (240 g) chicken or vegetable stock
- 1 cup (18 g) flat-leaf parsley leaves and tender stems, finely chopped
- 2 tablespoons (44 g) honey, or more to taste

seffa

- 14 ounces (2⅓ cups/396 g) couscous
- ¾ cup (150 g) golden or dark raisins, soaked in hot water for 15 minutes and drained
- 3 tablespoons (42 g) unsalted butter
- ½ teaspoon fine sea salt, or more to taste

1 Preheat the oven to 350°F (175°C). Spread the sliced almonds in a single layer on a baking sheet and toast in the oven, stirring the almonds or gently shaking the baking sheet halfway through for even baking, for 8 to 10 minutes, until golden. Remove from the oven and set aside. *(You can toast the almonds up to 3 days in advance and keep them in an airtight container.)*

2 Heat the olive oil and ghee or butter in a large pot over medium-low heat. Add the onions, cover the pot, and cook, stirring occasionally, until the onions are soft and translucent, 10 to 15 minutes.

3 Add the garlic, saffron, turmeric, ginger, cinnamon, salt, and pepper to the pot and cook, stirring frequently, until the mixture is fragrant, about 3 minutes. Add the chicken and stir to combine, then add the stock and parsley and bring to a boil over high heat. Reduce the heat to medium-low, cover the pot, and simmer for 40 to 45 minutes, until the chicken is cooked through. Using tongs or a slotted spoon, transfer the chicken to a chopping board and let cool slightly.

(recipe continues)

4 Add the honey to the pot, increase the heat to medium, and simmer for 20 to 30 minutes, stirring occasionally, until the sauce reduces and thickens; it should still have a pourable consistency.

5 Meanwhile, when the chicken is cool enough to handle, use a knife to slice it or shred it using two forks.

6 Return the chicken back to the pot and stir into the onion sauce. Taste and adjust the seasoning, adding more salt and/or honey if necessary. Let simmer over low heat, stirring occasionally while you make the couscous.

7 Cook the couscous according to the package instructions, or see Tip below for my trusted method. Then transfer to a bowl and mix in the raisins, butter, and salt. Taste and adjust the seasoning, adding more salt if necessary.

8 Spread about half of the couscous evenly over a large shallow serving plate. Spoon the onion and chicken mixture onto the couscous, toward the center of the plate. Sprinkle about three-quarters of the toasted almonds over the top. Spread the remaining couscous over the chicken mixture, using your hands or two large spoons to create a dome shape. Sprinkle on the remaining almonds and serve immediately.

TIP: This dish is traditionally made with s'men, fermented butter, but here I give the option of ghee, which is easier to find—or just use regular unsalted butter.

TIP: Preheat the oven to 350°F (175°C). In a baking dish, combine the couscous with cold or room-temperature vegetable stock (or water). Use your hands to make sure all the grains are evenly moistened. Let the couscous hydrate until all the liquid is absorbed, about 15 minutes. Then use a fork to fluff the couscous grains and check their consistency—they should be plump but still firm when pressed between two fingers. If the grains are still hard, add about ⅓ cup (80 g) more liquid and let sit for another 15 minutes before fluffing again. Once the couscous is hydrated, cover the dish tightly with foil and bake for 30 to 35 minutes, or until the couscous is tender and warmed through.

sheet-pan chicken with spiced grapes, chickpeas, and thyme

serves 4 to 6

Sheet-pan dinners are one of the tricks that I often turn to in order to make my life easier. To me, these recipes are about packing as many flavors and textures as possible onto one pan and letting the oven do its job. A roasted chicken may be the ultimate comfort food, and many of my sheet-pan dinners feature chicken. I love how the juices and fat that the chicken releases during the roasting process meld with the seasoning to create a rich, satisfying sauce. As soon as I take the pan out of the oven, I dip a big chunk of bread into the warm sauce—it is, without a doubt, the best part.

This recipe is a sheet-pan version of a grape, chickpea, and thyme chicken tagine. The grapes, added toward the end of cooking, caramelize in the hot juices and warm spices to create a delicious burst of flavor that beautifully complements the thyme. My favorite way to enjoy this dish is with a dollop of Greek yogurt and plenty of bread for sopping up the cooking juices.

- 2½ pounds (1133 g) bone-in, skin-on chicken breasts or thighs
- Fine sea salt
- ¾ cup (180 g) vegetable or chicken stock
- 3 tablespoons (45 g) olive oil, plus more for the pan and for drizzling
- 3 garlic cloves, minced or pressed
- 2 tablespoons chopped thyme, plus more for garnish
- 1½ teaspoons ground coriander
- 1½ teaspoons ground turmeric
- 1½ teaspoons ground ginger
- 1 teaspoon ground cumin
- 1 pound (453 g) yellow onions (2 large or 3 medium), thinly sliced
- One 15-ounce (425 g) can chickpeas, drained and rinsed
- 2 cups (300 g) seedless red or black grapes
- Flaky salt, such as Maldon, to serve (optional)

1 Preheat the oven to 425°F (220°C). Season the chicken pieces on both sides using ¾ teaspoon salt. Set aside.

2 *Make the marinade*: Combine the stock, olive oil, garlic, thyme, coriander, turmeric, ginger, cumin, and ¾ teaspoon salt in a small bowl and stir to mix.

3 Grease a baking sheet with olive oil. Add the onions, chickpeas, and about half of the marinade to the prepared pan, and toss to coat. Spread the onions and chickpeas out in the pan.

4 Add the chicken to the same bowl, pour the remaining marinade over it, and use your hands to thoroughly coat the chicken. Arrange the chicken skin side up on top of the onions and chickpeas and pour the marinade remaining in the bowl over the chicken; set the bowl aside.

5 Roast the chicken for 30 minutes, or until it starts to brown.

6 Meanwhile, add the grapes to the bowl you used for marinating, sprinkle with a generous pinch of salt, drizzle with olive oil, and toss to coat.

7 Remove the baking sheet from the oven and scatter the grapes around the chicken over the pan. Return to the oven and roast for another 10 to 15 minutes, until the chicken is fully golden and cooked through.

8 Garnish the chicken and chickpeas with thyme and flaky salt, if using, and serve immediately.

sheet-pan chicken with potatoes, preserved lemon, and olives

serves 4 to 6

This is one of Morocco's most popular tagines. I grew up eating it and countless variations of it, and for me, it always tastes like home. While there's definitely something special about the way this iconic dish is traditionally prepared, on busy weekdays I often turn to an easy sheet-pan version, which still allows me to enjoy all its flavors, from the citrusy brightness of preserved lemons to the savory depth of the brined olives. Plus, this recipe can easily be scaled up for serving larger groups if needed. After just 15 minutes of prep time, you simply pop everything onto a sheet pan and let the oven do the rest of the work.

- 3 tablespoons (45 g) olive oil, plus more for the pan
- 2½ pounds (1133 g) bone-in, skin-on chicken breasts or thighs
- 1½ teaspoons fine sea salt
- ¾ cup (180 g) vegetable or chicken stock
- 4 garlic cloves, minced or pressed
- 1 cup (18 g) flat-leaf parsley leaves and tender stems, finely chopped
- 1 cup (18 g) cilantro leaves and tender stems, finely chopped
- 1 tablespoon (20 g) seeded and finely chopped preserved lemons, homemade (page 41) or store-bought
- 1½ teaspoons ground turmeric
- 1½ teaspoons ground ginger
- ¼ teaspoon black pepper
- 1½ pounds (680 g) Yukon Gold or russet potatoes, peeled and cut into 1-inch (2.5 cm) pieces
- 1½ pounds (453 g) yellow onions, thinly sliced
- ½ cup (70g) pitted green olives, roughly torn or halved
- 1 lemon, thinly sliced
- Flaky salt, such as Maldon, to serve (optional)

1 Preheat the oven to 425°F (220°C). Grease a baking sheet with olive oil.

2 Season the chicken pieces on both sides using ¾ teaspoon salt. Set aside.

3 *Make the marinade*: Combine the stock, olive oil, garlic, parsley, cilantro, preserved lemon, turmeric, ginger, ¾ teaspoon salt, and the pepper in a medium bowl and stir to mix. Taste and add more chopped preserved lemon and/or salt, if desired.

4 Put the potatoes and onions in a large bowl, add half of the marinade, and toss to coat. Spread the potatoes and onions out on the prepared pan.

5 Add the chicken to the same bowl, pour the remaining marinade over it, and use your hands to thoroughly coat the chicken. Arrange the chicken skin side up on top of the onions and potatoes, and pour any marinade remaining in the bowl over the chicken, onions, and potatoes.

6 Roast for 30 minutes, or until the chicken and potatoes start to brown.

7 Take the pan out of the oven, scatter the olives around the chicken, and arrange the lemon slices on top of it. Return the pan to the oven and roast for another 10 to 15 minutes, or until the chicken and potatoes are golden and cooked through. Finish with flaky salt, if using, and serve immediately.

stuffed chicken with vermicelli and chicken liver–djaj maamer

serves 4

Weekends usually mean roast chicken in our home, a tradition I learned from my parents, and this recipe, a Moroccan classic, never disappoints. In Morocco, whole chickens come with all their giblets, including the liver, which usually goes straight into the stuffing. The vermicelli stuffing in this recipe includes a generous amount of fresh herbs along with preserved lemon. The liver adds richness and depth of flavor, but if you're not a fan of liver, just omit it, and you'll still have a delicious stuffing. I usually serve this with good bread for soaking up all the juices, but feel free to accompany it with rice or roasted potatoes or your own favorite side for roast chicken.

- 3 tablespoons (45 g) olive oil
- ½ teaspoon ground ginger
- ½ teaspoon ground turmeric
- ½ teaspoon sweet paprika
- 1 teaspoon fine sea salt
- ¼ teaspoon freshly black ground pepper
- One 4-pound (1812 g) whole chicken (reserve the liver if it is included)

stuffing

- 3 ounces (85 g) dried rice vermicelli, cooked according to the package instructions and drained
- ¼ cup (35 g) pitted green olives, finely chopped
- 1½ tablespoons olive oil
- 1 to 1½ tablespoons (20 to 30 g) seeded and finely chopped preserved lemons, homemade (page 41) or store-bought
- 1 cup (18 g) flat-leaf parsley leaves and tender stems, finely chopped
- 1 cup (18 g) cilantro leaves and tender stems, finely chopped
- 2 garlic cloves, minced or pressed
- ½ teaspoon ground ginger
- ½ teaspoon ground turmeric
- ½ teaspoon sweet paprika
- ¼ teaspoon fine sea salt, or more to taste
- ¼ teaspoon freshly black ground pepper
- 3 ounces (80 g) chicken livers, any membranes removed and chopped into ¼-inch (0.6 cm) pieces

- 2 large onions (440 g), roughly cut in into 1-inch (2.5 cm) wedges
- Green Harissa (page 47) to serve (optional)

1 Preheat the oven to 450°F (230°C). Combine the olive oil, ginger, turmeric, paprika, salt, and pepper in a small bowl. Pat the chicken dry with paper towels and use your hands or a brush to coat it inside and outside with the flavored oil. Set aside.

2 *Make the stuffing*: Combine the cooked vermicelli, olives, olive oil, 1 tablespoon chopped preserved lemon, parsley, cilantro, garlic, ginger, turmeric, paprika, salt, and pepper in a large bowl and mix well. Taste and adjust the seasoning, adding more salt and/or chopped preserved lemon by the teaspoon, if desired. Add the chicken liver and mix to combine.

3 Spoon the stuffing mixture into the cavity of the chicken and secure the opening with toothpicks. Arrange the onions in the center of a roasting pan and set the chicken on top. Pour enough water into the pan to reach a depth of about ¼ inch (0.6 cm).

4 Place the roasting pan in the oven and reduce the temperature to 400°F (205°C). Roast the chicken for 1¼ to 1½ hours, basting it every 20 minutes with the pan juices, until it is golden brown and cooked through; an instant-read thermometer inserted into the thickest part of a thigh should read 165°F (75°C). Remove from the oven and let the chicken rest for 10 minutes before carving.

5 Serve the chicken with the stuffing alongside the onions and some green harissa on the side, if desired.

chicken berkoukes soup

serves 4 to 6

Berkoukes, also known as m'hamsa, is a traditional North African pasta made from a combination of semolina and wheat flour. A staple of Moroccan, Algerian, and Tunisian cuisines, it is traditionally hand-rolled into tiny balls and then sun-dried. Outside North Africa, it may be referred to as pearl or giant couscous, although technically it qualifies more as pasta than couscous; in fact, I've found that acini di pepe makes a good substitute. With its unusual texture and ability to absorb flavors, berkoukes is used in various dishes in Morocco, particularly soups, with vegetables and meat, where it makes for a heartier dish. This recipe is a Moroccan rendition of the comforting chicken noodle soup found in many different cuisines around the world.

- 3 tablespoons (45 g) olive oil
- 2 medium carrots (200 g), cut into ½-inch (1.2 cm) dice
- 1 medium onion (170 g), cut into ½-inch (1.2 cm) dice
- 3 large celery stalks (100 g), cut into ½-inch (1.2 cm) dice
- 2½ tablespoons (37 g) tomato paste
- 2 garlic cloves, minced or pressed
- 1 teaspoon ground ginger
- 1 teaspoon ground turmeric
- 1 teaspoon sweet paprika
- 1½ teaspoons fine sea salt, or more to taste
- ¼ teaspoon black pepper, or more to taste
- 1 pound (453 g) skinless, boneless chicken thighs or breasts
- 5 cups (1200 g) chicken or vegetable stock
- 1 cup (170 g) pearl couscous
- 2 tablespoons (12 g) chopped cilantro leaves and tender stems for garnish

1 Heat the olive oil in a large pot over medium-low heat. Add the carrots, onions, and celery, cover, and cook, stirring occasionally, until the onions are soft and translucent, about 10 minutes.

2 Add the tomato paste, garlic, ginger, turmeric, paprika, salt, and pepper, stir everything together with a wooden spoon, and cook, stirring frequently, until the mixture is fragrant, 3 to 4 minutes.

3 Add the chicken and stock and bring to a boil over high heat. Cover the pot, reduce the heat to medium-low, and cook for 18 to 23 minutes, until the chicken is cooked through.

4 Use tongs or a slotted spoon to remove the chicken from the pot and transfer to a cutting board; set aside. Bring the stock back to a boil over medium-high heat, add the couscous or pasta, and cook for 10 to 12 minutes, or according to the package instructions, until tender.

5 Meanwhile, use two forks to shred the chicken into bite-size pieces, or slice it with a knife.

6 When the couscous is cooked, return the chicken to the pot. Taste and adjust the seasoning, adding more salt and/or pepper if necessary. Serve the soup immediately, garnished with the cilantro.

TIP: If the soup is not served straightaway, the couscous (or pasta) will continue to absorb the broth and become too soft. For this reason, I recommend not adding the couscous until right before serving time.

ⴰⴽⵙⵓⵎ
لحم

MEAT

kefta and rice-stuffed bell peppers with yogurt

serves 4

My mom used to make this dish frequently when we were growing up. She learned it from her friend Miriam, who lived next door to her in Fez. Miriam's family was Mizrahi, who are Jews from the Middle East and North Africa, and this meal was a staple for them on Shabbat. Interestingly, I also enjoyed a similar dish at my childhood friend Nilgun's home in Brussels, when her Turkish mom served her own version of stuffed peppers, with yogurt. Here is the recipe Miriam kindly passed down to my mom, and I also serve it with yogurt, just like Nilgun's mom. To me, this simple recipe, passed down through generations and across borders, exemplifies the unifying power of food and its ability to transcend cultures.

- 8 medium-large bell peppers (1360 g)
- ¼ cup (60 g) olive oil, plus more for drizzling
- 1 large onion (220 g), finely chopped
- 3 garlic cloves, minced or pressed
- 2½ teaspoons sweet paprika
- 2½ teaspoons ground cumin
- ¼ teaspoon ground cinnamon
- 1 pound (453 g) ground beef, 10 to 20% fat
- ¾ cup (200 g) canned crushed or diced tomatoes (half a 14-ounce/400 g can; use the other half for the sauce)
- 1 cup (160 g) cooked long-grain white rice
- ½ cup (120 g) vegetable stock or water
- 1 cup (18 g) flat-leaf parsley leaves and tender stems, finely chopped
- 1 cup (18 g) cilantro leaves and tender stems
- A handful of mint leaves, finely chopped
- 1 teaspoon fine sea salt, or more to taste
- ½ teaspoon black pepper

sauce

- ¾ cup (200 g) canned crushed or diced tomatoes (see above)
- ½ cup (120 g) vegetable stock or water
- 1 tablespoon tomato paste
- 2 garlic cloves, minced or pressed
- 1 teaspoon harissa, homemade (page 44) or store-bought, or more to taste (optional)
- ½ teaspoon fine sea salt, or more to taste
- Pinch of granulated sugar

- 1½ cups (360 g) Greek yogurt or whole-milk yogurt for serving

(recipe continues)

1 Preheat the oven to 400°F (205°C). Cut off the tops of the bell peppers and use a small spoon to carefully remove the seeds and white membranes from the insides of the peppers. Set the peppers and tops aside.

2 Heat 2½ tablespoons (37 g) of the olive oil in a large frying pan over medium-low heat. Add the onions, cover the pan, and cook, stirring occasionally, until the onions are soft and translucent, about 7 minutes.

3 Add the garlic, paprika, cumin, and cinnamon and cook, stirring occasionally, until fragrant, about 1 to 2 minutes. Add the ground meat, increase the heat to medium, and cook, breaking up the meat with a wooden spoon, until it is no longer pink, about 5 minutes.

4 Add the tomatoes, rice, stock or water, parsley, cilantro, mint, salt, and pepper, mix to combine, and adjust the seasoning, adding more salt if necessary. At this stage, the mixture should have a texture similar to that of risotto. If it's too dry, add a little stock or water a tablespoon at a time; if it's too liquid, cook for a couple of minutes to evaporate the excess liquid. Remove from the heat and set aside.

5 *Make the sauce*: Combine the tomatoes, stock or water, tomato paste, garlic, harissa, if using, salt, and sugar in a 13-×-9-inch (33 × 22 cm) baking dish and stir to mix. Taste and adjust the seasoning, adding more salt if necessary.

6 Fill the bell peppers with the beef-and-rice mixture and cover them with their tops. Arrange the filled peppers in the baking dish and drizzle with the remaining 1½ tablespoons (30 g) olive oil.

7 Cover the baking dish tightly with aluminum foil (if the bell pepper stems prevent a tight seal, simply cut them off) and bake for 30 to 35 minutes, until the peppers start to soften. Carefully remove the foil and bake for another 30 to 35 minutes, until the peppers are tender, charred, and a bit wrinkled; you should be able to pierce them easily with a knife.

8 Serve the peppers warm with the sauce, and the yogurt drizzled with olive oil on the side.

saffron beef chorba with crispy potatoes

serves 4 to 6

The word "chorba" refers to a clear soup traditionally seasoned with turmeric, ginger, and saffron. While it can be enjoyed throughout the year, it's often served during Ramadan to break the fast. This flavorful, versatile soup can be prepared with various proteins, including beef, chicken, or lamb. For this beef chorba, rather than cooking the potato chunks in the broth as it simmers, in the traditional way, I roast them separately until golden and crispy on the outside and tender on the inside. It's a simple twist that really enhances the soup by adding another texture and, as a result, comfort.

- 5 tablespoons (75 g) olive oil
- 2 medium yellow onions (340 g), chopped
- 1 tablespoon tomato paste
- 1½ teaspoons ground turmeric
- 1½ teaspoons ground ginger
- A large pinch of saffron threads (5 or 6 threads)
- ½ teaspoon black pepper, plus more to taste
- ¾ pound (340 g) boneless beef stewing meat, cut into 1-inch (2.5 cm) pieces
- 2 medium tomatoes (200 g), halved and grated on the large holes of a box grater, or finely chopped, with their juices
- 5½ cups (1320 g) vegetable stock or water
- Fine sea salt
- 1 pound (453 g) Yukon Gold or russet potatoes, peeled and cut into 1-inch (2.5 cm) pieces
- One 14-ounce (400 g) can chickpeas, rinsed and drained
- 3 ounces (85 g) spaghetti, broken into 1-inch (2.5 cm) pieces, or broken vermicelli
- Finely chopped flat-leaf parsley leaves and tender stems for garnish

1 Preheat the oven to 425°F (220°C). Line a large roasting pan or a baking sheet with parchment paper. Heat 2 tablespoons (30 g) of the olive oil in a Dutch oven or other large heavy pot over medium heat. Add the onions, tomato paste, 1 teaspoon each of the turmeric and ginger, the saffron, and pepper and cook, stirring frequently, until fragrant, about 2 minutes.

2 Add the beef and cook, stirring occasionally, until it is lightly browned on all sides, about 7 minutes.

3 Add the tomatoes, stock or water, and 1 teaspoon salt and bring to a boil over high heat. Reduce the heat to medium-low, cover, and simmer gently for about 1¼ hours, until the meat is cooked and breaks apart easily when pressed with a fork.

(recipe continues)

4 Meanwhile, after the chorba has simmered for about 30 minutes (so the potatoes and chorba will be finished at the same time), place the potato pieces in the lined roasting pan or on the baking sheet. Drizzle the remaining 3 tablespoons (45 g) olive oil over the potatoes and season with the remaining ½ teaspoon ginger and turmeric and ½ teaspoon salt. Use your hands to coat the potato pieces evenly with the spices and oil, and spread them out in the pan.

5 Transfer the potatoes to the oven and roast for 25 to 30 minutes, until they are golden and crispy on the outside and tender on the inside. Remove from the oven; if necessary, cover the potatoes loosely with foil to keep them warm while the chorba finishes cooking.

6 When the meat is cooked, and separates easily when pressed with a fork, add the chickpeas and broken pasta pressed to the chorba. Increase the heat and bring to a boil, then reduce the heat to low and simmer until the pasta is cooked, 7 to 10 minutes, or according to the package instructions.

7 If too much liquid has evaporated as the chorba cooked, add a ladleful of water or two to achieve the desired consistency. Taste and adjust the seasoning, adding more salt if necessary.

8 Serve the chorba in bowls, topped with the potatoes and parsley.

beef, potato, and olive tagine

serves 6

When I was growing up, my mother would prepare this tagine once a week for dinner, filling our home with the warm scents of cumin, ginger, paprika, and turmeric. A Moroccan classic, it is made with humble ingredients, but the slow-cooked beef becomes incredibly tender and infused with the rich spices. Now that I am a mother myself, I often make this tagine for my own family. It is traditionally served with bread, but my daughters and husband prefer it with jasmine rice.

- ¼ cup (60 g) olive oil
- 2½ pounds (1100 g) boneless beef chuck or other stewing beef, trimmed of excess fat and cut into 2-inch (5 cm) pieces
- 1 large onion (220 g), diced
- 3 garlic cloves, minced or pressed
- 1 teaspoon ground turmeric
- 1 teaspoon ground ginger
- 1 teaspoon sweet paprika
- ½ teaspoon ground cumin
- 3 medium tomatoes (300 g), halved and grated on the large holes of a box grater, or finely chopped, with their juices
- 1¼ cups (300 ml) vegetable stock or water, plus more if needed
- 1½ teaspoons fine sea salt, or more to taste
- 1½ pounds Yukon Gold or russet potatoes (679 g), peeled and cut into 1-inch-wide (2.5 cm) wedges
- 1 cup (140 g) drained pitted green olives
- Chopped cilantro leaves for garnish

1 Heat 2 tablespoons (30 g) of the olive oil in a Dutch oven or other large heavy pot over medium-high heat. Add the beef and cook, turning occasionally (wait until the meat releases easily from the bottom of the pot with a gentle lift using tongs), until nicely browned on all sides. Work in batches if necessary, as it's important not to overcrowd the pot; overcrowding can cause the meat to steam rather than sear. Once all the beef is browned, transfer it to a plate and set aside.

2 Reduce the heat to medium and add the remaining 2 tablespoons (30 g) olive oil. Add the onions, garlic, turmeric, ginger, paprika, and cumin and cook, stirring occasionally, until fragrant, about 1 to 2 minutes. Return the seared meat to the pot and add the tomatoes, vegetable stock or water, and salt. Increase the heat to medium-high and bring to a boil, then cover the pot, reduce the heat to low, and simmer until the meat is almost cooked and just starting to separate when pressed with a fork, 1¾ to 2 hours; stir every 20 minutes or so to prevent the sauce from sticking to the bottom of the pot.

3 Add the potato wedges to the pot, pushing them down into the liquid with a spoon. There should be enough liquid to almost cover the ingredients; if necessary, add a little more stock or water. Cover the pot and simmer until the potatoes are tender and cooked through, 20 to 25 minutes; move the potatoes around in the pot halfway through for even cooking.

4 Remove the lid, stir in the olives, and simmer for another 3 minutes. Taste and adjust the seasoning, adding more salt if necessary. Garnish with cilantro and serve immediately.

beef skewers with dill and lemon chermoula

serves 4

I like to think of dill and lemon chermoula as the Moroccan version of chimichurri, the popular Argentinean parsley and vinegar condiment traditionally served with grilled meats. The dill and lemon zest add a stronger citrusy fragrance and a different herbal kick to this classic marinade/sauce. If you can, plan ahead, as the longer the meat marinates in the chermoula, the more flavorful it will be. Serve these skewers with your side of choice, such as batbout (see 20-Minute Panfried Bread, page 86) and a mixed salad.

- 1¼ pounds (566 g) boneless beef sirloin or rump steak, cut into bite-size chunks
- ¾ cup (180 g) Dill and Lemon Chermoula (page 42)
- Bread and mixed salad to serve (optional)

1 If using bamboo skewers rather than metal ones, soak your skewers in water to cover for 30 minutes; drain.

2 Put the beef in a medium bowl or other container, add the chermoula, and turn to coat the beef. Cover and set aside for 15 minutes or refrigerate for up to 24 hours.

3 Prepare a medium-hot fire in a charcoal or gas grill, or preheat a griddle pan over medium-high heat. Thread the beef pieces onto the skewers.

4 Arrange the skewers on the grill or in the griddle pan and cook, turning a couple of times, for 2 to 4 minutes on each side until cooked, depending on your preferred level of doneness. Serve immediately with bread and a mixed salad if desired.

kefta and kale couscous bowls

serves 4

This recipe is my Moroccan version of a traditional Lao and Thai larb bowl. Here I use kefta, the flavorful Moroccan ground-meat mixture. The kefta is cooked with kale and served on a bed of couscous rather than the rice or noodles typically used for larb bowls. The couscous soaks up all the savory juices from the meat-and-kale mixture. The generous amounts of fresh herbs in the dish itself and the garnishes, along with the sliced red onion, bring more Moroccan flavors to the bowl.

This recipe cooks in less than 30 minutes, making it a great meal for a busy weeknight. Plus, it's convenient to prepare ahead of time, and it's easy to make in larger quantities. I often make a double recipe and portion it out into containers that I can then reheat throughout the week.

- ¼ cup (60 g) olive oil
- 1 medium yellow onion (170 g), finely chopped
- 1 pound (453 g) ground beef, 10 to 20% fat
- 2½ teaspoons sweet paprika
- 2 teaspoons ground cumin
- 1 cup (18 g) flat-leaf parsley leaves and tender stems, finely chopped
- 1 cup (18 g) cilantro leaves and tender stems, finely chopped, plus more for garnish
- A handful of mint leaves, roughly chopped, plus more for garnish
- Fine sea salt
- ½ teaspoon black pepper
- Pinch of cayenne pepper (optional)
- 4 cups (160 g) chopped kale (thick stalks removed)
- 2 cups (12 ounces/340 g) couscous
- 2 tablespoons (30 g) fresh lemon juice
- ½ small red onion (60 g), thinly sliced, for garnish

1 Heat 2 tablespoons of the olive oil (30 g) in a large frying pan over medium-low heat. Add the yellow onions, cover the pan, and cook, stirring occasionally, until the onions are soft and translucent, about 7 minutes.

2 Add the ground beef, paprika, and cumin and cook, breaking up the meat with the back of a wooden spoon, until it's no longer pink, 6 to 8 minutes.

3 Add the parsley, cilantro, and mint, then add 1 teaspoon salt, the black pepper, and cayenne pepper, if using, and stir to combine. Add the kale and mix it well with the meat. Cover the pan and cook, stirring occasionally, until the kale is tender, 5 to 8 minutes. Taste and adjust the seasoning, adding more salt if necessary. Remove from the heat.

4 Meanwhile, cook the couscous according to the package instructions. Transfer to a bowl, add the remaining 2 tablespoons olive oil, the lemon juice, and 1 teaspoon salt, or to taste, and mix well.

5 To serve, divide the couscous among four bowls, top with the kefta and kale, and garnish with the sliced red onions, cilantro, and mint leaves.

berber stuffed flatbreads—aghroum boutgouri

makes four 8-inch (20 cm) round stuffed flatbreads

Aghroum boutgouri is a stuffed Berber flatbread traditionally filled with a mixture of onions, ground meat, spices, and chopped herbs; it is most often served in the southern part of Morocco. The word "aghroum" means "bread" in Tamazight, the language spoken by the Amazigh (also known as the Berbers) across North Africa. It refers to a rustic flatbread, generally made from all-purpose flour, water, yeast, and salt. The dough is shaped into rounds, flattened, and cooked on a hot surface, such as a griddle or a skillet, giving the bread a slightly crispy texture on the outside and an irresistible soft and chewy texture inside.

While the harissa-and-yogurt sauce is optional, it comes together very quickly and is a great complement to the breads. I love to make these for dinner parties and serve them at the beginning of the meal. They tend not to last long, though, and I always regret not making more.

dough

- 4½ cups (480 g) all-purpose flour
- 1¼ teaspoons fine sea salt
- 1¼ teaspoons active dry yeast
- 1¼ cups (300 g) warm water
- 1½ tablespoons olive oil

filling

- 2 tablespoons (30 g) olive oil
- 2 medium yellow onions (340 g), chopped
- 1 medium red bell pepper (140 g), cored, seeded, and chopped into ½-inch (1.2 cm) pieces
- 1 medium green bell pepper (140 g), cored, seeded, and chopped into ½-inch (1.2 cm) pieces
- 1 cup (18 g) flat-leaf parsley leaves and tender stems, finely chopped
- 1½ teaspoons sweet paprika
- 1½ teaspoons ground cumin
- 1½ teaspoons fine sea salt, or more to taste
- ½ pound (227 g) ground beef, ideally 15% fat

harissa and yogurt sauce (optional)

- 3 tablespoons (45 g) whole-milk or Greek yogurt
- 1½ tablespoons (20 g) mayonnaise
- 1 teaspoon harissa, homemade (page 44) or store-bought, or more to taste

Olive oil for cooking the flatbreads

1 *Make the dough*: Combine the flour, salt, and yeast in a large bowl and mix together with a whisk or fork. Add the warm water and oil and stir with a rubber spatula until well combined. Use your hands to bring the mixture together, then knead until you have a smooth dough, about 5 minutes. Shape into a ball.

2 Lightly dust a work surface, turn the dough out, and knead it for 10 to 12 minutes, or until light and smooth. Alternatively, transfer the dough to the bowl of a stand mixer fitted with the dough hook and knead on low speed until the dough is light and smooth, about 8 minutes.

3 Transfer the dough to a large bowl, cover it with a kitchen towel, and let rise in a warm place for at least 30 minutes; the dough should expand noticeably, but it won't double in size.

(recipe continues)

4 *Make the filling*: Heat the olive oil in a large frying pan over low heat. Add the onions, cover the pan, and cook, stirring occasionally, until the onions are soft and translucent, about 10 minutes. Increase the heat to medium-low, add the bell peppers, parsley, paprika, cumin, and salt, and cook, stirring frequently, until the mixture is fragrant, 3 to 4 minutes.

5 Increase the heat to medium, add the ground meat, and cook, using a wooden spoon to break up the meat, until it is browned all over and any liquid has evaporated, 5 to 8 minutes. Remove from the heat, cover the pan, and let cool. *(You can prepare the filling up to 3 days in advance and keep it in a sealed container in the fridge.)*

6 *Make the sauce, if you'd like to serve it*: Combine the yogurt, mayonnaise, and harissa in a small bowl and stir together with a spoon. Taste and add more harissa, if desired. Cover the sauce and refrigerate until ready to serve. *(The sauce can be made ahead and kept in a sealed container in the fridge for up to 3 days.)*

7 *Fill the breads*: Punch the dough down and turn it out onto a floured surface. Divide it into 8 equal pieces and shape each one into a ball. Work with 1 piece of dough at a time, keeping the other balls covered with a kitchen towel.

8 Dust your rolling pin with flour and flatten a dough ball into a 6-inch (15 cm) disk. Spoon ¼ of the filling onto the dough, leaving a border of about ½ inch (1.2 cm) all around. Flatten another dough ball into a 6-inch (15 cm) disk and place on top of the first one, making sure that the edges of the rounds are aligned. Seal the edges of the dough by folding the edges of the bottom disk over the edges of the top one, pressing the dough gently together. Dust the filled bread on both sides with flour and use the floured rolling pin to flatten and roll the filled bread into an 8-inch (20 cm) disk. Transfer the bread to a tray dusted with flour and cover with a kitchen towel. Repeat the process with the remaining dough and filling to make 3 more breads.

9 *Cook the breads*: Heat 1 tablespoon olive oil in a large heavy frying pan or griddle over medium-low heat until hot. Carefully transfer one of the breads to the pan and cook until it is starting to brown on the bottom, 1 to 2 minutes. Flip the bread over and continue to cook, flipping the bread every 1 to 2 minutes, until it is cooked through and golden on both sides, 6 to 8 minutes. Transfer to a plate and cover with a cloth to keep warm while you cook the remaining breads. Cook the remaining breads, wiping out the pan between batches to remove any cooked flour and adding more oil as needed.

10 Serve immediately, with the sauce, if you made it.

TIP: For a cheater's version of this recipe, use 4 store-bought flatbreads. Spread ¼ of the filling on one side of each one, fold the bread in half, and cook as instructed above.

beef short ribs with prunes

serves 6

These ribs are inspired by the classic meat-and-prune tagine m'qualli ("m'qualli" refers to the seasoning mixture used in the sauce), part of the culinary heritage of many Moroccan families. This tagine, which may be made with meat or chicken, is often served at celebratory events such as weddings or religious ceremonies, or to celebrate the birth of a child. For falling-off-the-bone tenderness, the ribs are first seared on the stovetop until well browned. Then they're transferred to the oven to braise slowly in a fragrant prune sauce made with onions, garlic, cilantro, and a warm spice blend of turmeric, ginger, and cinnamon. The sauce is finished with prunes and just a bit of honey for a hint of sweetness.

- 2 large (450 g) yellow onions, chopped into large chunks
- ½ pound (227 g) soft pitted prunes, halved lengthwise
- 5 tablespoons (75 g) olive oil
- 1½ cups (330 g) vegetable or beef stock
- 4 large garlic cloves
- 2 teaspoons ground turmeric
- 2 teaspoons ground ginger
- ¾ teaspoon ground cinnamon
- 1 cup (18 g) cilantro leaves and tender stems, plus more for garnish
- 1 teaspoon fine sea salt, plus more for seasoning the ribs
- ½ teaspoon black pepper
- 5 pounds (2200 g) beef short ribs cut into 3-inch (7.6 cm) lengths
- 2½ tablespoons (55 g) honey
- 2 tablespoons toasted sliced almonds for garnish

1 *Make the prune sauce*: Combine the onions, half of the prunes, 2 tablespoons (30 g) of the olive oil, the stock, garlic, turmeric, ginger, cinnamon, cilantro, salt, and pepper in a food processor or blender and process until you have a smooth sauce. Set aside.

2 Preheat the oven to 350°F (175°C). Season the ribs with salt. Heat the remaining 3 tablespoons (45 g) oil in a Dutch oven or other large heavy pot over medium-high heat. Working in batches to avoid overcrowding, so that the ribs will sear rather than steam, add the ribs to the pot and cook, turning occasionally, until browned on all sides, about 8 to 10 minutes; transfer the ribs to a platter or large bowl as they are done. Drain off all but about 2 tablespoons of the fat from the pot.

3 Return all the browned ribs, along with any accumulated juices, to the Dutch oven, pour the prune sauce over them, and bring to a boil over high heat. Cover the pot, carefully transfer to the oven, and cook until the ribs are falling-apart tender, 2½ to 3 hours. Some of the bones may have separated from the meat at this stage; just remove and discard them. Transfer the short ribs to a large serving plate and cover with foil.

(recipe continues)

4 Skim off most of the fat from the sauce and transfer the sauce to a small saucepan. Add the honey and bring to a boil over medium-high heat, then reduce the heat to medium-low and cook for 10 minutes, or until the sauce has reduced by half, again skimming any excess fat from the surface. Stir in the remaining prunes and cook over low heat for about 2 minutes, or until they are heated through. Taste the sauce and adjust the seasoning, adding more salt and/or honey, if desired.

5 Remove the foil from the platter, pour the sauce over the ribs, and garnish with the roughly chopped cilantro and sliced almonds. Serve immediately.

TIPS: If your prunes are hard, soak them in warm water to cover for 20 minutes; drain them before using.

You can prepare this dish a day ahead and refrigerate the ribs and sauce in separate containers. When ready to serve, reheat the ribs on a baking sheet, covered with foil, in a 350°F (175°C) oven for 15 to 20 minutes. Meanwhile, reheat the sauce in a saucepan over low heat. If the sauce is too thick, loosen it with a tablespoon or so of water or stock to achieve the proper consistency.

likama smash cheeseburgers with smoky harissa sauce

serves 4

Everyone loves a good burger, and I am lucky enough to live in London, where the options for burgers are almost endless. I like to try as many types of burgers as I can, and much to my surprise, I've recently found myself falling in love with the smash burger. For years, my favorites were the ones with thicker patties sometimes referred to as "bistro-style burgers." Somehow, I'd thought that smash burgers were not as special and were mostly for kids. I was very wrong. The smashed, thinner patties have a larger surface area of caramelized meat, resulting in more flavor and a better cheese-to-meat ratio. Moreover, they can hold garnishes better than thicker burgers, making them easier to pick up and to bite into. This recipe is my homage to the smash burger. The patties are seasoned with likama, a classic Moroccan spice blend, and a piquant sauce made with harissa and smoked paprika stands in for the usual ketchup.

smoky harissa sauce

- 1/3 cup (73 g) mayonnaise
- 1 tablespoon (22 g) harissa, homemade (page 44) or store-bought, or more to taste
- 1 tablespoon ketchup
- 2 teaspoons yellow mustard
- 1 1/4 teaspoons smoked paprika

- 1 1/2 pounds (680 g) ground beef, at least 20% fat
- 1 1/4 tablespoons Likama Spice Blend (page 37)
- 4 soft burger buns, split
- 1 to 2 tablespoons (15 to 30 g) vegetable oil
- Fine sea salt and black pepper to taste
- 8 slices cheddar or American cheese
- 1/2 large yellow onion (110 g), sliced into rings

1 *Make the sauce*: Combine the mayonnaise, harissa, ketchup, mustard, and smoked paprika in a medium bowl. Set aside. *(You can prepare the sauce in advance and keep in a sealed container in the fridge for up to 5 days.)*

2 Combine the ground meat and likama in a large bowl and use your hands or a large tablespoon to mix the spices into the meat. Divide the meat into 8 portions and roughly roll each one into a ball. Do not try to shape the meat into perfect balls; handling it too much will result in dense patties. Set aside.

3 Heat a large frying pan, preferably cast iron, or griddle over medium heat. Add the buns cut side down (in batches if necessary) and toast until the bottoms start to turn golden brown around the edges, 1 to 2 minutes. Transfer to a plate.

4 Add 1 tablespoon of oil to the pan and increase the heat to high. Make sure that the pan is hot before you start cooking the meat. Add only as many balls of meat as fit comfortably in the pan, keeping in mind that they will be flattened and need space between them. (Cook the patties in batches if necessary, adding more oil as needed.) Use a large metal spatula to quickly press down each portion of meat to form a patty that is slightly larger than the diameter of the bun. (The meat will shrink during cooking, so this will allow you to end up with patties that are roughly the same size as the buns.) Season the patties with salt and pepper and cook until they are seared on the bottom and a brown crust has developed, about 2 minutes. Slide the spatula under each burger, making sure you get all the caramelized parts, and flip. Season the top of the patties with salt and pepper and lay a slice of cheese on each one. Cook until the bottom of the patties is caramelized, the meat is cooked to your liking, and the cheese has melted. Top each of 4 patties with one of the remaining patties and transfer to a plate.

5 Spread a tablespoon of the harissa sauce on each cut side of the toasted buns, place 2 stacked patties on each bottom bun, and top each with 2 to 3 onion rings and a bun top. Serve immediately.

cumin and preserved-lemon beef stew–tangia marrakchia

serves 6

If you've ever wandered around the bustling Jemaa el-Fna souk in Marrakech, you will have noticed tangia pots stacked in many of the food stalls. These distinctive tall clay pots, a hallmark of the city, also lend their name to the meat stew known as "tangia." Traditionally the pots are filled with meat, spices, preserved lemon, garlic, and s'men, a fermented butter (here I've substituted ghee or unsalted butter for convenience), sealed with parchment paper and string, and then nestled in the ashes of a wood-burning fire, either at a local hammam (public bath house) or ferran (old-fashioned public oven), where the tangia slow-cooks to perfection. The result is buttery, falling-apart meat infused with warm aromas. To prepare this contemporary version that holds true to the spirit of a traditional tangia, you can use a Dutch oven or a slow cooker.

- ⅔ cup (160 g) beef stock or water, plus more if needed
- 3 tablespoons (45 g) olive oil
- 6 garlic cloves, minced or pressed
- 1 tablespoon ghee or melted unsalted butter
- A very large pinch of saffron threads (about a dozen threads)
- 1 tablespoon ground cumin, plus more for serving
- ½ teaspoon fine sea salt, plus more for serving
- 2 small preserved lemons (50 g), homemade (page 41) or store-bought
- 3 pounds (1300 g) boneless beef shanks or chuck roast, cut into 1½- to 2-inch-thick (3.8 to 5 cm) slabs
- Finely chopped flat-leaf parsley leaves and tender stems for garnish
- Bread for serving
- Tomato salad, for serving (optional)

1 If you are using a Dutch oven, preheat the oven to 325°F (160°C). Add the beef stock or water, olive oil, garlic, ghee or butter, saffron, cumin, and salt to the Dutch oven or a slow cooker and whisk to combine.

2 For a strong preserved-lemon flavor, seed and finely chop enough of the lemons, both flesh and rind, to make 2 tablespoons and stir into the stock mixture. For a milder preserved-lemon flavor, cut the lemons into quarters, discard the seeds, and add the lemon quarters to the mixture. Add the meat to the Dutch oven or slow cooker and use your hands to coat it thoroughly.

3 If using a Dutch oven, cover it, transfer to the oven, and cook for 4 hours, or until the meat is extremely tender and falls apart easily; check the pot every 45 minutes and add more stock or water if necessary, aiming for about ½ to 1 inch of liquid. If using a slow cooker, cook on low for 8 hours.

4 Transfer the meat and juices to serving plates. Garnish with parsley and serve with bread and tomato salad, if desired.

TIP: For extra flavor, ask your butcher for some beef bones and add them to the Dutch oven or slow cooker along with the other ingredients before cooking the tangia.

lamb tagine with carrots and peas

serves 6

The combination of carrots and peas is popular with most children, and this classic lamb tagine always reminds me of my childhood. Back then, I wasn't a big fan of lamb, so my mom would always pile my plate high with the scented carrots and tender peas. But the magic of this tagine lies in how the flavors of the savory lamb and the spices mingle with the sweetness of the vegetables, something that I have long come to appreciate. Serve this with crusty bread, couscous, or your grain of choice, and don't forget to add a final squeeze of lemon juice to the dish to brighten all its flavors.

- ¼ cup (60 g) olive oil
- 2¼ pounds (1019 g) boneless lamb neck or lamb stew meat (leg or shoulder, or a combination), trimmed of excess fat and cut into 2- to 3-inch (5 to 7.6 cm) pieces
- 1 large onion (220 g), diced
- 3 garlic cloves, minced or pressed
- 1 teaspoon ground turmeric
- 1 teaspoon ground ginger
- ½ teaspoon sweet paprika
- ½ teaspoon ground cumin
- 1 cup (240 g) vegetable stock or water, plus more if needed
- 2 medium tomatoes (200 g), halved and grated on the large holes of a box grater, or finely chopped, with their juices
- 1 cup (18 g) flat-leaf parsley leaves and tender stems, chopped, plus more for garnish
- 1¼ teaspoons fine sea salt, or more to taste
- ¾ pound (340 g) carrots (about 3 medium), peeled and cut into ½-inch (1.2 cm) dice
- 1½ cups (200 g) peas
- Lemon wedges or for serving

1 Heat 2 tablespoons (30 g) of the olive oil in a Dutch oven or other large heavy pot over medium-high heat. Working in batches if necessary to avoid crowding the pot (which would cause the meat to steam rather than sear), add the lamb and cook, turning occasionally (wait until the meat releases naturally from the bottom of the pot before turning the pieces), until nicely browned on all sides. As the lamb is browned, transfer it to a plate.

2 Reduce the heat under the pot to medium and add the remaining 2 tablespoons (30 g) olive oil. Add the onions, garlic, turmeric, ginger, paprika, and cumin and cook, stirring occasionally, until fragrant, 1 to 2 minutes.

3 Return the seared meat to the pot and add the stock or water, tomatoes, parsley, and salt. Increase the heat to medium-high and bring to a boil, then cover the pot, reduce the heat to low, and simmer until the meat is almost cooked (it should be starting to separate easily when pressed with a fork), 1¾ to 2 hours; stir every 30 minutes or so to prevent the sauce from sticking to the bottom of the pot.

4 Add the carrots to the pot, pushing them down into the liquid with a spoon. There should be enough liquid to nearly cover all the ingredients but not fully submerge them; if necessary, add more stock or water. Cover the pot and simmer until the carrots are tender, 15 to 20 minutes. The lamb should be fully tender and separate easily when pressed with a fork.

5 Remove the lid, stir in the peas, and simmer until they are cooked, about 5 minutes. Taste and adjust the seasoning, adding more salt if necessary.

6 Remove the pot from the heat, garnish the tagine with chopped parsley, and serve with lemon wedges on the side.

lamb covered in tomatoes and onions—tagine maqfoul

serves 6

"Maqfoul" means "locked" in Moroccan Arabic, and it is a nod to the way the tagine is prepared. The meat is nestled underneath a generous layer of sliced onions and tomatoes, which lock in its moisture and infuse it with the aromatic flavors of ground ginger, turmeric, and cinnamon. I used to be intimidated by the thought of making this tagine, and I'd wait for visits to Morocco to enjoy it at my parents' or aunties' houses. But I've learned that mastering the dish is more about patience and planning than complexity. It's one of my favorite meals for hosting when I need something special, yet it requires minimal time and attention since it's mostly hands-off. Serve it with lots of warm bread to soak up the juices and the fragrant, almost caramelized, jamlike tomatoes and onions.

You can prepare the tagine up to 2 days in advance, let it cool, and refrigerate. When ready to serve, reheat it, covered, in a 350°F (175°C) oven for about 30 minutes.

- 3 tablespoons (45 g) olive oil
- 1 large yellow onion (220 g), finely chopped
- 4 garlic cloves, minced or pressed
- 1½ teaspoons ground turmeric
- 1 teaspoon ground ginger
- ½ teaspoon ground cinnamon
- Pinch of saffron threads (optional)
- 1½ teaspoons fine sea salt, or more to taste
- ¼ teaspoon black pepper
- 3 pounds (1360 g) boneless lamb neck or lamb stew meat (leg or shoulder, or a combination), trimmed of excess fat and cut into 2- to 3-inch (5 cm to 7.6 cm) pieces
- A small bouquet of cilantro sprigs, tied together with kitchen twine
- ½ cup (120 g) vegetable stock or water
- 2 tablespoons (44 g) honey, or more to taste

maqfoul layer

- 4 medium yellow onions (680 g), cut into ¼-inch-thick (0.6 cm) slices
- 4 medium tomatoes (400 g), cut into ¼-inch-thick (0.6 cm) slices
- Generous pinch of fine sea salt
- Generous pinch of ground cinnamon
- 1½ teaspoons honey

- 1½ tablespoons (15 g) toasted sesame seeds (optional)

1 Heat the olive oil in a large, deep, ovenproof frying pan, ideally a heavy-bottomed 10-inch (25 cm) pan with a lid, over medium-low heat (you can use a Dutch oven if you don't have a large deep skillet). Add the chopped onions, garlic, turmeric, ginger, cinnamon, saffron, if using, salt, and pepper and cook, stirring frequently, until the onions have begun to soften, about 3 minutes.

2 Add the lamb, increase the heat to medium, and cook, stirring occasionally, until it is lightly browned, about 7 minutes. Add the cilantro bouquet, stock or water, and honey and bring to a boil over high heat.

3 Cover the pan, reduce the heat to low, and simmer for 1 to 1½ hours, until the lamb has partially softened; when pressed with a fork it should be tender but not falling apart. Use tongs to remove the cilantro bouquet and discard it. Taste the broth and adjust the seasoning, adding more salt or honey if necessary.

(recipe continues)

4 Preheat the oven to 350°F (175°C). *Add the maqfoul layer to the pan*: Transfer 6 tablespoons of the broth from the pan to a small bowl and set aside. Arrange the onion slices on top of the lamb pieces so they cover them fully. Drizzle 3 tablespoons of the reserved broth over the onions. Arrange the tomato slices on top of the onions and drizzle the remaining broth over the tomatoes. Sprinkle the tomatoes with the salt and cinnamon and drizzle the honey over the top.

5 Cover the pan with a lid, transfer to the oven, and cook for 40 to 45 minutes, until the onion slices are very tender.

6 Remove the lid, return the pan to the oven, and cook for another 20 to 30 minutes, until the sauce has thickened slightly (aim for a sauce that coats the back of a spoon), the onions and tomatoes are lightly browned, and the lamb falls apart easily when pressed with a fork. If your sauce is too thin at this point, return the pan to the oven, uncovered, and cook for another 15 to 30 minutes. Or, if the sauce has the right consistency but the lamb isn't falling-apart tender, cover the pan and return to the oven for another 20 to 30 minutes.

7 Remove the tagine from the oven, garnish with the sesame seeds, if using, and serve.

TIP: For a very caramelized result, when the tagine is done, place the pan under the broiler for about 5 minutes, until the tomatoes and onions are lightly charred.

hasselback butternut squash with merguez and walnut

Merguez are spicy sausages from North Africa or, more particularly, the Maghreb region, which includes Algeria, Morocco, Tunisia, and Libya. Made from ground lamb or beef, or a combination of both, they are heavily spiced with cumin, sweet paprika, and cayenne pepper or harissa. In this dish, the smoky, savory sausage is an ideal counterpoint to the sweet, nutty squash. But perhaps the beauty of the dish lies in the fact that it makes an unusual and beautiful centerpiece for a special meal that requires little attention or effort.

Hasselback potatoes are a classic Swedish dish made with potatoes that are sliced in a way that creates a fanlike effect, drizzled with melted butter, and roasted until the edges of the slices are crisp and the centers are meltingly soft. Here, I use the same technique for preparing butternut squash and then drizzle the squash generously with spiced olive oil; as the squash bakes, the individual slices absorb all the flavors of the marinade while they brown and crisp up in the oven. Serve couscous alongside for a comforting North African–inspired meal.

serves 4 to 6

1 small butternut squash (1133 g)

marinade

- 2 tablespoons (30 g) olive oil
- ½ teaspoon ground turmeric
- ½ teaspoon ground cumin
- ½ teaspoon sweet paprika
- ¾ teaspoon fine sea salt
- ¼ teaspoon black pepper

mint oil

- ½ cup packed mint leaves
- ⅓ cup (80 g) olive oil
- Generous pinch of granulated sugar
- ¼ teaspoon fine sea salt, or more to taste
- ⅛ teaspoon black pepper, or more to taste

merguez and walnut topping

- 4 garlic cloves, minced or pressed
- 1 tablespoon (22 g) harissa, homemade (page 44) or store-bought (optional)
- 2 tablespoons sweet paprika
- 1½ tablespoons ground cumin
- 1½ tablespoons ground coriander
- 1 tablespoon ground fennel
- 1½ teaspoons dried mint
- 1½ teaspoons granulated sugar
- ½ teaspoon cayenne pepper (optional)
- 1 teaspoon fine sea salt, or more to taste
- ½ teaspoon black pepper
- 1 pound (453 g) ground beef, 15 to 20% fat, or lamb, or, ideally, a combination of both
- 2 tablespoons (30 g) olive oil
- ¾ cup (85 g) chopped walnuts

(recipe continues)

1 Preheat the oven to 400°F (205°C). Slice the squash lengthwise in half and use a vegetable peeler to remove the skin. Use a large spoon to scrape out the seeds and membranes.

2 Place the squash halves cut side down on a baking sheet and bake for 20 minutes, or until the squash is soft enough to slice into. Remove from the oven and let cool for 10 minutes.

3 *Meanwhile, make the marinade*: Combine the olive oil, turmeric, cumin, paprika, salt, and pepper in a small bowl and stir well. Set aside.

4 Place one squash half cut side up on a cutting board and slice crosswise into ⅛-inch-thick (0.3 cm) slices without cutting all the way through the squash, stopping ¼ to ½ inch (0.6 to 1.2 cm) from the skin (to help prevent the knife from cutting all the way through the squash, you can slide two chopsticks under the long sides of the squash). Repeat with the other squash half.

5 Return the squash to the baking sheet, cut side up, drizzle the marinade evenly over the it, and use your hands or a brush to spread it all over the flesh and in between the slices. Transfer the squash to the oven and roast for 25 to 30 minutes, until fork-tender and lightly browned.

6 *Make the mint oil*: Combine the mint, olive oil, sugar, salt, and pepper in a food processor and pulse until the mint is finely chopped and the mixture is smooth. Alternatively, finely chop the mint and combine with the olive oil, sugar, salt, and pepper in a small bowl, mixing well. Taste and adjust the seasoning, adding more salt and/or pepper, if desired. Set aside.

7 *Make the merguez and walnut topping*: Combine the garlic, harissa, if using, paprika, cumin, coriander, fennel, mint, sugar, cayenne, if using, salt, and pepper in a large bowl. Add the ground meat and use your hands or a large spoon to mix it with the spices. Cover and refrigerate until ready to use.

8 About 15 minutes before the squash is done, start cooking the topping, so both are ready at the same time. Heat ½ tablespoon of the olive oil in a large frying pan over medium heat. Add the chopped walnuts and cook, stirring frequently, until lightly toasted, 3 to 5 minutes. Transfer the walnuts to a small bowl and set aside.

9 Add the remaining 1½ tablespoons olive oil to the pan, add the merguez mixture, and cook, breaking up the meat with the back of a wooden spoon, until it's browned and cooked through, about 8 minutes. Add the walnuts and mix to combine. Taste and adjust the seasoning, adding more salt if necessary. Remove from the heat.

10 Use two large spatulas to transfer the roasted squash halves to a large serving plate. Top each one with several large spoonfuls of the topping and spoon the remaining topping around the squash. Drizzle the mint oil over all and serve.

spiced meatballs with rice–kefta "bil harsh"

serves 4

My parents, who immigrated to Brussels before I was born, were originally from Fez. As a result, most of the Moroccan meals I enjoyed while growing up were Fassi dishes, originating in the Fez region. But several times a year, my mom and I would travel to Rabat, the capital of Morocco, to visit her relatives, and there I learned about Rabati food as well. Kefta bil harsh was one of the new dishes I learned about on these visits. "Bil harsh" means "with harshness," or "coarseness," which refers to the texture rice adds to the meatballs and to the little "spikes" that appear on the surface of the meatballs when they are cooked. Simmered in a richly spiced onion sauce, these tender meatballs make an excellent option for large gatherings. The recipe can easily be doubled (make the sauce in two pans), and everyone–children and adults alike–loves meatballs.

- 3 tablespoons (45 g) olive oil
- 3 medium onions (510 g), finely diced
- 2 garlic cloves, minced or pressed
- 1½ teaspoons ground turmeric
- 1½ teaspoons ground cumin
- ½ teaspoon ground cinnamon
- Pinch of granulated sugar
- 1 cup (18 g) flat-leaf parsley leaves and tender stems, finely chopped, plus more for garnish
- 1 cup (18 g) cilantro leaves and tender stems, finely chopped
- 1 cup (240 g) vegetable stock or water
- Fine sea salt
- 1 pound (453 g) ground beef, 15 to 20% fat
- ½ cup (105 g) basmati rice
- 1 medium egg, beaten
- Bread for serving

1 Heat the olive oil in a large frying pan over medium heat. Add about two-thirds of the onions, the garlic, ¾ teaspoon of the turmeric, ¾ teaspoon of the cumin, ¼ teaspoon of the cinnamon, and the sugar and cook, stirring frequently, until the mixture is fragrant, 3 to 4 minutes.

2 Add about half of the parsley and cilantro, the stock or water and ½ teaspoon salt, and bring to a boil over high heat. Cover the pan, reduce the heat to low, and simmer for 30 minutes, stirring occasionally to make sure the onions don't stick to the bottom of the pan, or until the onions are soft and translucent and infused with the flavors of the spices. The sauce may have thickened slightly, but the pan should not be dry; if necessary, add more stock or water a tablespoon at a time until there is about ½ inch of sauce in the pan. Taste and adjust the seasoning, adding more salt if necessary.

3 *Meanwhile, make the meatballs*: Combine the beef, rice, egg, the remaining onion, the remaining parsley and cilantro, the remaining ¾ teaspoon turmeric, ¾ teaspoon cumin, ¼ teaspoon cinnamon, and ¾ teaspoon salt. Use your hands or a large spoon to mix all the ingredients together. Shape the mixture into 1½-inch meatballs about the size of a golf ball (about 40 g); you should have about 18 meatballs. Arrange on a plate, cover, and refrigerate. *(The meatballs can be made ahead and stored in a sealed container in the fridge for up 24 hours.)*

4 When the onion sauce is ready, increase the heat to medium-low, add the meatballs to the pan, cover, and cook for 8 minutes. Remove the lid and use tongs or a large spoon to flip the meatballs, then cover the pan again and cook for another 8 minutes. At this stage, the meatballs should be cooked through and the rice should be tender; if that's not the case, turn off the heat, cover the pan, and let stand for 5 to 7 minutes. The residual heat will finish cooking the meatballs.

5 Garnish the meatballs with parsley and serve with bread.

ras el hanout lamb shoulder méchoui with pistachio and apricot salsa

serves 6 to 8

I was lucky enough to grow up in a home where we often had lots of company and family around—which meant lots of people to feed. On those occasions, if my mom wanted to make something special that required minimal effort, she served a roasted lamb shoulder. After all, roasts actually follow a concept similar to sheet-pan dinners; the main ingredients—here, the meat and lots of onions—are combined in a pan and the oven does most of the work. In Morocco, "méchoui" can refer to either grilled or roasted dishes, but for a lamb shoulder, it typically means that it is roasted. This lamb shoulder, infused with ras el hanout and then slow-cooked, is guaranteed to be the star of any gathering. Serve it with couscous, roasted potatoes, or good bread.

- One 4½-pound (2000 g) bone-in lamb shoulder roast
- 3 medium onions (510 g), quartered
- 3 tablespoons (45 g) olive oil
- 5 garlic cloves, minced or pressed
- 1½ tablespoons ras el hanout, preferably homemade (page 38)
- 1¼ teaspoons fine sea salt
- ½ teaspoon black pepper
- ½ to ¾ cup (120 to 180 g) chicken or vegetable stock

pistachio and apricot salsa

- 1 small red onion (120 g), finely chopped
- ⅔ cup (106 g) shelled pistachios, chopped or crushed
- ⅔ cup (120 g) dried apricots, finely chopped
- 1½ cups (27 g) cilantro leaves and tender stems, finely chopped
- ¼ cup (60 g) olive oil
- 2 tablespoons (30 g) white wine vinegar
- ½ teaspoon fine sea salt, or more to taste
- ½ teaspoon ground black pepper

1 Preheat the oven to 350°F (175°C). Pat the lamb dry with paper towels and use a small sharp knife to pierce the flesh all over on both sides, about 20 times.

2 Arrange the onions in the center of a large roasting pan and place the lamb on top.

3 Combine the olive oil, garlic, ras el hanout, salt, and pepper in a small bowl and stir until well mixed. Pour the oil-and-spice mixture all over the lamb shoulder, turning to coat it on both sides, and then use your hands or a brush to spread it all over the lamb, making sure that you work it into the incisions as well. Keep the roast fat side up.

4 Pour enough stock into the roasting pan to reach a depth of about ¼ inch (0.64 cm) and cover it tightly with foil. Transfer the pan to the oven and roast for 3½ to 4 hours, basting the meat every hour with the juices until the meat is tender.

5 Carefully remove the foil from the pan (don't discard it) and roast the lamb for 35 to 45 minutes longer, or until the skin is crisp and golden and the meat is very tender and falling off the bone. Remove the pan from the oven, cover the lamb loosely with the reserved foil, and let the lamb rest for 20 minutes.

6 *Meanwhile, make the salsa*: Combine the red onion, pistachios, apricots, cilantro, olive oil, vinegar, salt, and pepper in a small bowl.

7 When the lamb has rested, carve it and serve immediately with the onions and pan juices, garnished with the salsa.

ⴰⵙⵍⵎ
سمك

FISH

AND SEAFOOD

"tayb o'hari" chickpeas, tuna, and egg salad

serves 4

Tayb o'hari is a popular street food made with dried chickpeas soaked in water, simmered until soft, and delicately seasoned with ground cumin, sweet paprika, and just a touch of cayenne pepper. It always brings back childhood memories of summers spent in Morocco, when I'd hold my mother's hand tightly as we wandered around Fez's Old Town, listening to her chat with the vendors and stopping for snacks along the way. Tayb o'hari was one of her favorite street foods, and when she made it at home, she always added extra cayenne and salt, as I do today. For this recipe, I was inspired to add tayb o'hari to a tuna salad, which is garnished with soft-boiled eggs and a sprinkling of paprika and cumin, classic Moroccan spices.

- 2 tablespoons (30 g) olive oil, plus more for drizzling
- 1 tablespoon red wine vinegar
- ½ teaspoon fine sea salt
- 2 5-ounce (142 g) cans tuna (preferably oil-packed), drained
- Half a medium red onion (85 g), finely diced
- ⅓ cup (43 g) drained pitted green olives, quartered lengthwise
- 2 large eggs, at room temperature

chickpeas

- 2 tablespoons (30 g) olive oil
- One 14-ounce (396 g) can chickpeas, drained and rinsed
- 1 teaspoon ground cumin, plus more for sprinkling
- 1 teaspoon sweet paprika, plus more for sprinkling
- ½ teaspoon fine sea salt
- ¼ teaspoon cayenne or other chile powder (optional)

- 2 cups (50 g) arugula
- ½ cup (9 g) cilantro leaves
- Lemon halves, to serve

1 Combine the olive oil, vinegar, and salt in a medium bowl and stir to blend. Add the tuna, onions, and olives and stir to mix. Set aside. *(The tuna can be prepared up to 2 days ahead and stored in a sealed container in the fridge.)*

2 Bring a small saucepan of water to a boil. Gently add the eggs to the boiling water, reduce the heat, and simmer for 6 minutes for soft-boiled eggs (if you prefer your eggs cooked more, simmer for 8 minutes for medium-cooked eggs, or 12 minutes for hard-boiled eggs). Drain the eggs and transfer to a bowl of ice water for 5 minutes to stop the cooking process, then drain and peel.

3 *Make the chickpeas*: Heat the olive oil in a large frying pan over low heat. Add the chickpeas, cumin, paprika, salt, and cayenne, if using, and cook until the chickpeas are softened and warm, 5 to 7 minutes. Remove from the heat. *(The chickpeas are best served warm, but they can be served at room temperature.)*

4 Arrange the arugula on a large serving plate, scatter the cilantro and marinated tuna over it. Scatter the chickpeas around the tuna. Arrange the soft-boiled eggs on top of the salad and carefully slice them. Drizzle the salad with olive oil and squeeze the lemon halves over the top. Sprinkle paprika and cumin over the eggs and serve.

TIP: This recipe also works with cannellini or butter beans instead of chickpeas.

shrimp m'hammer tagine

serves 4 to 6

Among the wide variety of Moroccan tagines, m'qualli and m'hammer are the most common. Both have an onion-sauce base with garlic and herbs, but their seasoning differentiates them. M'qualli tagines are seasoned with ground turmeric and ginger, resulting in a yellow-brownish sauce, while the sauces for m'hammer tagines, seasoned with cumin and sweet paprika, are reddish-brown. Both versions are commonly prepared with beef, lamb, or chicken, but I'd always wondered why they were never made with seafood, and I decided to experiment with a shrimp m'hammer tagine. The result is a deeply flavorful and satisfying tagine with a classic onion sauce, often considered the best part of a m'hammer tagine.

- ¼ cup (60 g) olive oil
- 2 large yellow onions (440 g), thinly sliced
- 3 garlic cloves, minced or pressed
- 1 tablespoon sweet paprika
- 2 teaspoons ground cumin
- ½ teaspoon ground turmeric
- 1 cup (18 g) cilantro leaves and tender stems, finely chopped
- ¾ cup (180 g) vegetable stock or water, plus more if necessary
- ¾ teaspoon fine sea salt, plus more to taste
- ¼ teaspoon black pepper
- 1 pound (453 g) medium or large shrimp, peeled and deveined
- 1 tablespoon toasted sliced almonds (optional)

1 Heat the olive oil in a large frying pan over medium-low heat. Add the onions, cover, and cook, stirring occasionally, until the onions are soft and translucent, 10 to 15 minutes.

2 Add the garlic, paprika, cumin, and turmeric and cook, stirring occasionally, until fragrant, about 2 minutes. Add the cilantro, stock or water, salt, and pepper and bring to a boil over high heat. Cover the pan, reduce the heat to low, and cook gently for 1 hour, stirring every 15 to 20 minutes to prevent the onions from sticking.

3 At this point, the sauce should have thickened slightly, its color should be slightly darker, and its flavor mellow; if that's not the case, let the sauce cook for another 15 minutes or so. The longer it cooks, the more depth and flavor it will have. If it looks as if there isn't enough liquid in the pan at any point, add more stock or water a tablespoon or so at a time. If it looks as if there isn't enough liquid in the pan at any point, add more stock or water, a tablespoon or so at a time, as necessary. Conversely, if it seems there is too much liquid and the sauce isn't thick enough to coat the back of a spoon, uncover the pan and cook, stirring occasionally, for 10 to 15 minutes to reduce it.

4 Taste the sauce and adjust the seasoning, adding more salt if necessary. Add the shrimp to the simmering sauce, stir to coat, and cook until the shrimp turn pink and are cooked through, about 4 to 6 minutes. Remove from the heat.

5 Garnish the tagine with toasted sliced almonds, if desired, and serve.

chermoula salmon with quick-pickled cucumbers

serves 6

This recipe pairs the vibrant flavors of chermoula, the classic marinade traditionally used in Morocco to season whitefish such as sea bass, with the richness of salmon for a delicious and easy meal. The quick-pickled cucumbers, which are ready by the time the fish is off the heat, add a refreshing note of acidity and sweetness. This dish is easy enough for weeknight dinners but impressive enough for a dinner party. I recommend serving the salmon with a green salad and a hearty Moroccan potato salad (Cumin-and-Parsley Potato Salad, page 94). The recipe also works with individual fish fillets and other types of whitefish, such as cod or halibut, though you may need to adjust the cooking time according to the thickness of the fish.

- 1 small English cucumber (½ pound/226 g), thinly sliced
- ½ medium red onion (85 g), thinly sliced
- ¾ teaspoon fine sea salt
- ¾ teaspoon granulated sugar
- 1½ tablespoons (22 g) white wine vinegar
- 1¾ -pound (793 g) skin-on salmon fillet or fillets
- ½ cup (100 g) Classic Chermoula (page 38)
- Toasted sesame seeds, to serve (optional)
- Green salad, to serve (optional)

1 Combine the cucumber, red onion, salt, sugar, and white wine vinegar in a medium bowl and mix well. Cover and set aside.

2 Line a baking sheet with parchment paper. Pat the salmon dry with paper towels and place it skin side down on the sheet. Pour the chermoula over the salmon, spreading it so it coats the entire surface evenly. If desired, before roasting, cover and marinate the salmon in the fridge for 1 or up to 24 hours, for a deeper flavor.

3 Preheat the oven to 350°F (175°C). Place the salmon in the oven and bake for 12 to 15 minutes, until it is cooked through and flakes easily with a fork. The cooking time may vary depending on the thickness of your fish; reduce the time if you prefer the fish less well cooked. Remove from the oven.

4 Drain the pickled cucumbers and onions in a sieve and scatter over the top of the salmon. Serve immediately with a sprinkle of sesame seeds and a green salad on the side, if desired.

seafood bastilla pie with caramelized tomatoes

serves 6

While the chicken version of bastilla, the classic sweet-and-savory pie (Quick Chicken Bastilla Puff Pies, page 153), is more widely known outside Morocco, its seafood variation is perhaps equally popular within the country. But the choice between the two versions can spark heated family discussions, especially when the question is which one to serve for a celebration. I actually love both equally, but for everyday meals I have a slight preference for a seafood bastilla, because it is lighter and requires less time to prepare. For this particular seafood bastilla, instead of enclosing the filling in phyllo pastry as in the traditional version, the filling is cooked in an ovenproof skillet and then topped with crumpled phyllo sheets before baking the pie. The scrunched-up phyllo sheets gives the bastilla a beautiful appearance while providing the classic crunch and, most importantly, they speed up the preparation process.

The pie is a real treat on its own, but the caramelized tomatoes (known as maticha maasla in Morocco) takes it to another level. It's packed with concentrated flavors like umami, tartness, and a hint of sweetness, as well as a subtle floral aroma from the saffron. You can choose to skip it, but it takes only minutes to prepare, and I encourage you to make it.

- 3 tablespoons (45 g) olive oil
- 2 large yellow onions (440 g), sliced
- 1 medium red bell pepper (140 g), cored, seeded, and cut into ½-inch (1.2 cm) pieces
- 3 garlic cloves, minced or pressed
- 2½ teaspoons sweet paprika
- 1½ teaspoons ground cumin
- 1¼ teaspoons fine sea salt, or more to taste
- ¼ teaspoon black pepper
- ½ pound (226 g) skinless cod fillet (any pin bones removed), cut into 1-inch (2.5 cm) pieces
- ½ pound (226 g) small or medium shrimp, peeled, deveined
- ½ pound (226 g) cleaned squid bodies, cut into 1-inch (2.5 cm) pieces
- 1 to 2 tablespoons (20 to 40 g) seeded and finely chopped preserved lemons, homemade (page 41) or store-bought
- 2 cups (36 g) flat-leaf parsley leaves and tender stems, finely chopped
- 2½ tablespoons (37 g) fresh lemon juice, or more to taste
- 3 ounces (85 g) rice vermicelli, cooked according to the package instructions, drained, rinsed under cold water, and roughly cut into 2-inch (2.5 cm) pieces
- 5 or 6 phyllo sheets
- 4 tablespoons (56 g) unsalted butter, melted
- 1½ cups (320 g) Caramelized Tomatoes (page 48)

(recipe continues)

1 Preheat the oven to 400°F (205°C). Heat the olive oil in a large (10-inch/25 cm) cast-iron or other heavy ovenproof frying pan over low heat. Add the onions, cover the pan, and cook, stirring occasionally, until the onions are soft and translucent, 10 to 15 minutes.

2 Add the bell pepper, garlic, paprika, cumin, salt, and pepper, reduce the heat to medium-low, and cook, stirring occasionally, until the onions start to caramelize, 10 to 15 minutes.

3 Add the cod, shrimp, squid, 2 teaspoons preserved lemon, parsley, and lemon juice. Cook for a minute and turn off the heat. Stir in the vermicelli then taste and adjust the seasoning, adding more preserved lemon, lemon juice, and/or salt if necessary.

4 Lay a phyllo sheet out on your work surface and brush with melted butter, then loosely scrunch it up and place on top of the filling. Repeat with the remaining sheets until the pie is fully covered with phyllo pastry. Bake for 30 to 35 minutes, or until the filling is hot and the pastry is golden.

5 Remove the pie from the oven and serve immediately, with the maticha maasla on the side.

fish "meatballs" and tomato tagine

serves 4

There's something incredibly comforting about meatballs of any type: the aroma that fills the kitchen as they simmer in a rich tomato sauce is simply irresistible, and with their tender texture, they practically melt in your mouth. This tomato tagine with fish "meatballs" originated in the northern part of Morocco, along the Atlantic coast. The meatballs, seasoned with cumin, sweet paprika, and parsley, make an interesting change from classic meatballs, and the flaky cooked fish gives them a lighter but still satisfying texture.

- 2 tablespoons (30 g) olive oil
- 1 medium onion (170 g), grated or finely chopped
- 2 garlic cloves, minced or pressed
- 1½ teaspoons sweet paprika
- 1 teaspoon ground cumin
- One 14-ounce (396 g) can crushed tomatoes
- 1 cup (18 g) flat-leaf parsley leaves and tender stems, finely chopped, plus more for garnish
- ½ teaspoon fine sea salt, or more to taste
- ½ teaspoon granulated sugar
- ¼ teaspoon black pepper

fish meatballs

- 1 pound (453g) skinless whitefish fillets, such as cod, haddock, or halibut, roughly chopped
- 1 large egg, beaten
- ⅓ cup (50 g) dried breadcrumbs
- 1 cup (18 g) flat-leaf parsley leaves and tender stems, roughly chopped
- 1½ tablespoons olive oil
- 2 garlic cloves, minced or pressed
- 1¼ teaspoons sweet paprika
- 1¼ teaspoons ground cumin
- 1 teaspoon fine sea salt, or more to taste
- ½ teaspoon black pepper
- Pinch of ground cinnamon

Lemon wedges for serving

Bread for serving

1 Heat the olive oil in a large frying pan over medium-low heat. Add the onions, cover the pan, and cook, stirring occasionally, until the onions are soft and translucent, about 7 minutes.

2 Add the garlic, paprika, and cumin and cook, stirring occasionally, until fragrant, about 1 to 2 minutes. Add the crushed tomatoes, parsley, salt, sugar, and pepper, increase the heat to medium-high, and bring to a boil.

3 Cover the pan, reduce the heat to low, and simmer for 35 to 40 minutes, until the sauce is fragrant and its texture velvety; stir every to 10 to 15 minutes to prevent the sauce from sticking to the bottom of the pan. If it looks as if the sauce is too dry at any point, add a couple of tablespoons of water.

(recipe continues)

4 *Meanwhile, prepare the fish meatballs*: Combine the fish, egg, breadcrumbs, parsley, olive oil, garlic, paprika, cumin, salt, pepper, and cinnamon in the bowl of a food processor (preferably a large one) and process until well blended and smooth.

5 To check the seasoning of the fish mixture, shape a teaspoon of it into a small ball and cook it in the microwave, or in a small frying pan with a drizzle of olive oil. Taste it, and add more salt to the rest of the mixture if necessary.

6 Shape the mixture into 1½-inch (3.8 cm) balls (you should have 16 or 17 meatballs). Set aside on a plate.

7 When the tomato sauce is ready, taste and adjust the seasoning, adding more salt if necessary. Add the meatballs to the pan, cover, and cook for about 6 minutes, until they start to firm up. Flip the balls, cover the pan, and simmer until they are cooked through, about 6 minutes.

8 Garnish the tagine with parsley and serve with lemon wedges and bread.

jalapeño shrimp tagine "pil pil"

serves 4

Northern Morocco shares part of its border with some of the small Spanish territories in North Africa, which has resulted in an interesting culinary exchange over centuries that is evident in many dishes. "Pil pil" is a Spanish term for a cooking technique, often used for seafood, where the ingredients are sautéed in olive oil with garlic and chile peppers until they release their flavors into a rich sauce. Moroccans have adapted that technique for a version of a classic shrimp-and-tomato tagine. Here quick-pickled jalapeños are added at the end of cooking for tartness, heat, and color. Serve the tagine with crusty bread for scooping up the delicious sauce.

pickled jalapeños

- 2 tablespoons (30 g) white wine vinegar
- 2 teaspoons granulated sugar
- ½ teaspoon fine sea salt
- 4 jalapeños (80 g) or other mild to medium-hot green chiles, thinly sliced

- 3 tablespoons (45 g) olive oil, plus more for drizzling
- 1 medium yellow onion (170 g), grated or finely chopped
- 3 garlic cloves, minced or pressed
- 1 tablespoon (15 g) tomato paste
- 1½ teaspoons sweet paprika
- 1 teaspoon ground cumin
- 3 medium tomatoes (300 g), halved and grated on the large holes of a box grater, or finely chopped, with their juices
- ½ cup (120 g) vegetable stock or water, or more if needed
- 1 cup (18 g) flat-leaf parsley leaves and tender stems, finely chopped
- ½ teaspoon granulated sugar
- ¾ teaspoon fine sea salt, or more to taste
- ¼ teaspoon black pepper
- ¼ teaspoon cayenne pepper, or more to taste (optional)
- 1 pound (453 g) medium or large shrimp, peeled and deveined

1 *Make the pickled jalapeños*: Combine the vinegar, sugar, and salt in a small bowl and stir to mix. Add the jalapeños, stir well, cover, and set aside.

2 Heat the olive oil in a large frying pan over medium-low heat. Add the onion, garlic, tomato paste, paprika, and cumin and cook, stirring occasionally, until fragrant, 1 to 2 minutes.

3 Add the tomatoes, stock or water, parsley, sugar, salt, black pepper, and cayenne, if using, and bring to a simmer. Cover the pan, reduce the heat to low, and simmer until the sauce is fragrant, its texture has become more velvety, and it has slightly reduced, 35 to 40 minutes; stir every 10 to 15 minutes to prevent the sauce from sticking to the bottom of the pan.

4 Add the shrimp and stir to coat; if the tomato sauce is too thick to coat the shrimp well, add a few tablespoons of stock or water. Cook until the shrimp are pink and opaque throughout, 4 to 6 minutes.

5 Spoon the pickled jalapeños over the tagine, drizzle with olive oil, and serve immediately.

almond and herb-crusted cod with t'faya

serves 4

Made with caramelized onions, plump raisins, honey, and cinnamon, T'faya (page 51) is a favorite Moroccan condiment, rich, warm, sweet, and savory. It is traditionally used as a topping or an accompaniment for a classic couscous dish, but its complex flavors make it a welcome addition to many other dishes as well, such as roasted chicken, or an unusual sandwich spread. Here it adds aromatic notes to the cod fillets, which are topped with a crunchy almond-and-panko-crumb mixture. The recipe comes together surprisingly quickly but offers a multitude of flavors in every bite.

- ⅓ cup (40 g) panko breadcrumbs
- ⅓ cup (33 g) sliced almonds
- 1½ tablespoons finely chopped flat-leaf parsley leaves and tender stems
- 1 tablespoon olive oil, plus more for drizzling
- Fine sea salt
- 4 cod fillets (5 to 7 ounces/141 to 198 g each), with or without skin, patted dry
- Black pepper
- ¾ to 1 cup (262 to 350 g) T'faya (page 51)
- Lemon wedges, to serve

1 Preheat the oven to 400°F (205°C). Line a baking sheet with parchment paper. Combine the panko, almonds, parsley, olive oil, and ½ teaspoon salt in a small bowl. Set aside.

2 Season the cod fillets on both sides with salt and pepper. Place skin or skinned side down on the lined baking sheet and drizzle with olive oil. Top each fillet with 3 to 4 tablespoons of the t'faya. Sprinkle the top of the fillets generously with the almond-and-panko mixture, then scatter any remaining crumbs around the fillets.

3 Bake for 10 to 12 minutes, or until the fish is cooked through and the crumb topping is golden. Serve immediately with lemon wedges.

seafood berkoukes

serves 4

This recipe was inspired by a dish typically served in seafood restaurants in Morocco. Customers order their seafood of choice to be either grilled or deep-fried, and it usually comes with an array of small side dishes like salads, fries, and often a turmeric-infused rice dish. I often replace the rice with berkoukes, tiny semolina pasta balls (also known as pearl or giant couscous) and stir the cooked shrimp and squid into it. The result is a dish that is somewhat similar to a paella, and like Spanish bomba rice, berkoukes absorb the seafood stock, infusing every bite with flavor. For a more flavorful broth, consider making your own fish stock (see Tip). It will take a bit of extra time, but it's absolutely worth it.

- ¼ cup (60 g) olive oil, plus more for drizzling
- 2 medium onions (340 g), finely chopped
- 1½ cups (255 g) pearl couscous
- 2 garlic cloves, minced or pressed
- 1¼ teaspoons ground turmeric
- ¾ teaspoon sweet paprika
- Pinch of saffron threads
- Fine sea salt
- 1 medium red bell pepper (140 g), cored, seeded, and cut into ¼-inch (0.6 cm) dice
- 1¾ cups (420 g) seafood or vegetable stock, plus more if needed
- ½ pound (226 g) cleaned squid bodies, cut into ½-inch (1.2 cm) rings
- ½ pound (226 g) small or medium shrimp, peeled and deveined
- ¼ teaspoon black pepper
- About 2 cups (50 g) arugula for serving
- 4 lemon wedges for serving

1 Heat 3 tablespoons (45 g) of the olive oil in a large frying pan over medium-low heat. Add the onions, cover the pan, and cook, stirring occasionally, until soft and translucent, about 7 minutes.

2 Meanwhile, put the couscous in a fine-mesh sieve, hold it under a gentle stream of very cold running water, and, using your fingers or a spoon, gently stir the couscous to rinse it thoroughly and remove any excess starch; once the water running through the sieve remains clear, drain the couscous and set aside.

3 Add the garlic, 1 teaspoon of the turmeric, ½ teaspoon of the paprika, the saffron, and ½ teaspoon salt to the onions and cook, stirring occasionally, until fragrant, about 1 to 2 minutes. Add the diced red pepper and cook, stirring occasionally, until soft, about 5 minutes.

4 Add the couscous and stock, stir to combine, and bring to a boil over high heat. Cover the pan, reduce the heat to medium-low, and simmer, stirring occasionally, until the couscous (or pasta) has softened but it is still slightly firm to the bite, about 10 to 12 minutes. If all the liquid has been absorbed but the couscous (or pasta) is not yet cooked, add more stock or water about ¼ cup (60 g) at a time until it is ready.

5 Meanwhile, heat the remaining tablespoon of olive oil in a frying pan over medium heat. Add the squid, shrimp, the remaining ¼ teaspoon each turmeric and paprika, ¼ teaspoon salt, and the black pepper and cook, stirring frequently, until the squid is firm and opaque and the shrimp are pink and cooked through, 3 to 5 minutes.

6 Transfer the shrimp and squid to the pan of couscous and mix to combine. Taste and adjust the seasoning, adding more salt if necessary.

7 Serve the berkoukes warm on a large plate or individual plates. Top with some arugula and a drizzle of olive oil, and place the lemon wedges on the side.

TIP: To make seafood stock for this recipe, simmer the shrimp shells in 2 cups (480 g) water for 20 minutes. Strain and use as instructed.

ⵜⴰⵙⵓⵎⵙⴰⵜ
حلويات

SWEET TREATS

pistachio jawhara cups

serves 4

Jawhara, also known as milk bastilla or k'tefa in Morocco, is a cherished celebratory dish and the dessert counterpart to a chicken or a seafood bastilla. With its layers of pastry and custard, jawhara is somewhat reminiscent of a French mille-feuille, but it sets itself apart with a lighter, airier texture, thanks to the delicate phyllo pastry and gently set orange blossom custard. It can be prepared as individual portions or as a grand cake. When we were growing up, my mother used to make a large jawhara for my brothers and me for Eid al Fitr, the holy celebration that marks the end of Ramadan, and we looked forward to it every year. In this version, crumbled baked caramelized phyllo dough and ground pistachios give the dish a special touch.

orange blossom custard

- 2¼ cups (540 g) whole milk
- 4 large egg yolks
- ¼ cup (50 g) granulated sugar
- 3 tablespoons (28 g) cornstarch
- 1 teaspoon orange blossom water, or more to taste
- Generous pinch of ground cinnamon
- 2 tablespoons (28 g) unsalted butter

phyllo crumble

- 4 large sheets phyllo pastry (9 by 14 inches/23 by 35 cm)
- 8 tablespoons (113 g) unsalted butter, melted
- ¼ cup (50 g) granulated sugar

pistachios

- ¾ cup (120 g) shelled pistachios
- 1½ tablespoons granulated sugar
- Pinch of fine sea salt

1 *Make the custard*: Heat the milk in a medium saucepan over medium heat just until it starts to simmer, with small bubbles around the edges. Remove from the heat.

2 Whisk the egg yolks, sugar, cornstarch, orange blossom water, and cinnamon together in a large bowl until smooth.

3 Add the warm milk to the egg mixture ¼ cup (60 g) at a time, whisking vigorously until well combined. Return the mixture to the saucepan and cook over medium-low heat, stirring constantly, until the custard is thick enough to coat the back of a spoon, 5 to 8 minutes. Turn off the heat, add the butter, and whisk until it has melted. Taste and adjust the flavor, adding more orange blossom water, if desired.

4 Cover the custard with plastic wrap, pressing the plastic directly against the surface to keep a skin from forming, and let cool to room temperature. If you won't be using the custard within 2 hours, cover and refrigerate until ready to assemble the dessert. *(You can prepare the custard up to 2 days in advance and keep it in an airtight container in the fridge.)*

(recipe continues)

5 *Prepare the phyllo crumble*: Preheat the oven 350°F (175°C), with a rack in the center. Place a phyllo sheet on a large baking sheet. (If your phyllo sheets are larger than the pan, use scissors to trim them to fit.) Brush generously with some of the melted butter and sprinkle 1 tablespoon of the sugar evenly over the phyllo. Place another phyllo sheet on top of the first one, brush with butter, and sprinkle evenly with another tablespoon of the sugar; set aside. Repeat with the remaining phyllo, butter, and sugar on a second baking sheet. (You can bake the first sheet of phyllo while assembling the second one but keep a careful eye on it.)

6 Transfer one of the baking sheets to the oven and bake for 5 to 10 minutes, until the phyllo is golden brown. The sugar-covered phyllo sheet will brown very quickly, so keep an eye on it to make sure it doesn't burn. (Don't be tempted to bake both pans at the same time–they will not bake evenly.) Remove the pan from the oven and let cool until you can comfortably handle the phyllo, at least 7 minutes. Bake the second pan of phyllo and let cool slightly.

7 Break the baked phyllo into pieces and add them to a large bowl. Use your hands to crush them into ¼-to-1-inch (0.6 to 2.5 cm) pieces. Cover the bowl with plastic wrap or transfer the phyllo to an airtight container and set aside. *(The crumble can be prepared up to 2 days in advance.)*

8 *Prepare the pistachios*: Combine the pistachios, sugar, and salt in a food processor and process until the nuts are coarsely ground. Transfer to an airtight container and set aside. *(The pistachios can be kept in an airtight container at room temperature for up to 3 days.)*

9 When ready to serve, gently reheat the custard in a small saucepan over low heat, stirring frequently, until just warmed through. Fill each of four small jars, tumblers, or cups with ¼ cup of the phyllo crumble, 3 to 4 tablespoons of warm custard, and 1 tablespoon ground almonds, then top with another layer of pastry and an additional 3 to 4 tablespoons of custard. Garnish each with ground pistachios and serve immediately.

TIP: Use the leftover egg whites to make Almond Macaroons (page 268).

moroccan mint tea chocolate cheesecake

makes one 9-inch cheesecake; serves 8

When I moved to the UK, I quickly noticed that Brits love the combination of chocolate and mint. The first time I enjoyed a mint and chocolate Magnum ice cream bar was during my first year in London. When I embarked on my culinary journey a few years later, I began experimenting with infusing various creams with Moroccan mint tea, and naturally, chocolate found its way into the mix. This creamy mint tea chocolate cheesecake is a testament to my passion for creating indulgent delights that tell a story.

mint tea chocolate cream

- ¾ cup (180 g) heavy cream
- ½ cup (120 g) whole milk
- 2 tablespoons (11 g) loose gunpowder green tea
- ½ cup (20 g) tightly packed mint leaves
- ¾ pound (340 g) semisweet or bittersweet chocolate, finely chopped, or store-bought bag of mini-chips (about 2 cups)
- 1 teaspoon vanilla extract

crust

- 4 tablespoons (57 g) unsalted butter, melted, plus softened butter for the pan
- 24 Oreos (270 g)
- 1 tablespoon unsweetened cocoa powder

filling

- 21 ounces (595 g) cream cheese, at room temperature
- 1 cup (200 g) granulated sugar
- 3 large eggs, at room temperature
- ½ teaspoon fine sea salt
- ¼ cup (33 g) all-purpose flour

1 *Infuse the cream mixture*: Combine the cream and milk in a small saucepan and bring just to a simmer over medium-low heat. Remove the pan from the heat and stir in the tea and mint leaves. Cover the pan and set aside to steep for 30 to 60 minutes. The longer you leave it to steep, the stronger the mint tea flavor will be.

2 *Meanwhile, make the crust*: Lightly grease a 9-inch (23 cm) springform pan with butter and line with parchment paper, pressing the paper firmly against the bottom of the pan; set aside. Combine the Oreos and cocoa powder in a food processor and process to fine crumbs. Add the melted butter, processing briefly until the crumbs are evenly moistened. Transfer the crumbs to the prepared pan and press them firmly over the bottom. Set aside.

3 *Finish the chocolate cream*: Strain the cream and milk mixture through a fine-mesh sieve into a medium bowl, pressing on the solids to release as much liquid as possible; discard the tea and mint leaves. Return the infused cream to the saucepan and set over low heat. Add the chocolate and vanilla and heat, stirring, for about 2 to 3 minutes, until the chocolate has melted and the mixture is smooth. Remove the pan from the heat and let the cream cool until it is just tepid. (To speed up the process, transfer the mixture to a bowl and place in the fridge for 5 minutes.)

(recipe continues)

4 Preheat the oven to 350°F (175°C).

5 *Make the filling*: In the bowl of a stand mixer fitted with the paddle attachment, or in a large bowl, using an electric handheld mixer, combine the cream cheese and sugar and beat until smooth and fluffy, about 2 minutes.

6 Add the eggs one at a time, beating until each egg is thoroughly incorporated before adding the next; scrape the bottom and sides of the bowl if necessary. Beat in the salt, then slowly pour in the chocolate cream, beating until it is thoroughly incorporated and the mixture is smooth and airy, about 1 minute. Add the flour and beat until just incorporated.

7 *Bake the cheesecake*: Place the springform pan on a baking sheet (to contain any overflow or leakage) and pour the filling into the pan; smooth the top. Transfer to the oven and bake for 55 to 60 minutes, until the cheesecake is puffed up but is still slightly jiggly in the center when the pan is shaken gently.

8 Remove from the oven and allow the cheesecake to cool in the pan for at least 1 hour. It will firm up and deflate slightly as it cools.

9 Release the sides of the pan and, using the parchment paper, slide the cheesecake onto a serving plate. Let cool completely before slicing and serving.

10 The cheesecake can be stored tightly covered or in a sealed container at room temperature for up to 24 hours or in the fridge for up to 3 days.

TIP: HOW TO MAKE MOROCCAN MINT TEA:

If you don't have a Moroccan teapot, you can prepare the tea in a saucepan.

When preparing traditional Moroccan mint tea, the first step is to extract the essence of the tea leaves and wash them. Place a small amount of gunpowder green tea (1 to 2 tablespoons, depending on the size of the pot) into a Moroccan teapot. Pour in about ½ cup (120 g) boiling water and let it sit for 30 seconds. Then pour this first infusion (in other words, the liquid without the leaves), known as the tea's "essence," into a cup and set aside.

Next, rinse the tea leaves by adding another ½ cup (120 g) boiling water to the teapot. Let steep for about 60 seconds, swirl the pot a couple of times, then discard the liquid. Return the reserved essence to the teapot and add fresh mint leaves and sugar, and enough boiling water to fill the pot.

Place the teapot over medium-low heat, allowing the mint to fully infuse its aromatic flavor. The tea is ready when it comes to a boil and steam begins to escape from the lid.

When pouring the tea into glasses or cusp, use a fine-mesh strainer to catch any loose leaves.

molten chocolate olive oil cake

serves 6

Olive oil isn't often used in French baked goods, especially chocolate ones, but sometimes the most unlikely combinations turn out to be the most special. In this recipe, the olive oil, used instead of butter, brings a delicate lightness and subtle flavor to the rich, decadent cake, which has a molten chocolate center and a crisp crust. I like to serve this for special occasions, but because it comes together in no time, I often prepare it right after dinner and let it bake while we take a break before dessert. Like many chocolate cakes, it's best enjoyed with a side of vanilla ice cream, but don't skip the drizzle of olive oil and sprinkling of salt on top, another unlikely yet delicious combination.

- ½ cup (120 g) olive oil, plus more for the pan and for drizzling
- ½ pound (226 g) semisweet chocolate, chopped
- ⅔ cup (133g) granulated sugar
- 4 large eggs
- ⅓ cup (40 g) all-purpose flour
- ¼ teaspoon fine sea salt
- 1 teaspoon vanilla extract
- Flaky salt, such as Maldon, to serve
- Vanilla ice cream for serving

1 Preheat the oven to 350°F (175°C). Grease an 8-inch (20 cm) cast-iron or other heavy ovenproof frying pan with olive oil.

2 Put the olive oil and chocolate in a microwave-safe bowl and microwave for 15-second intervals, stirring after each one, until melted and smooth.

3 Using a handheld electric mixer, beat the sugar and eggs on high speed in a large bowl until the mixture is light and fluffy, pale, and increased in volume, about 3 to 4 minutes. Add the flour and salt and beat until well incorporated. Add the melted chocolate mixture and vanilla and beat until well combined, about 1 minute.

4 Pour the batter into the prepared pan and place it in a large sheet pan. Fill the sheet pan with warm water until it reaches about halfway up the sides of the sheet pan. Carefully place the sheet pan in the oven, making sure not to spill the water. Bake for 22 to 26 minutes, until the cake has developed a crust on top and a toothpick inserted in the edge of the cake comes out with some small moist crumbs and another inserted in the middle comes out wet. Remove the cake from the oven and let cool for at least 5 minutes before serving.

5 Sprinkle flaky salt over the cake. Serve warm or at room temperature with vanilla ice cream and a little drizzle of olive oil over the ice cream.

TIP: You can make the batter in advance and pour it into the pan, then cover and refrigerate until ready to bake. When ready to serve, transfer the pan to the oven and bake for 28 to 32 minutes.

brown sugar, apple, and orange blossom cobbler with brown butter topping

serves 6

This recipe is my nostalgic, Moroccan-inspired take on a Speculoos dessert. Speculoos (a version of the Dutch speculaas, and found in the UK in a brand named Biscoff), is a popular Belgian cookie from the Flanders region, not far from Brussels, where I grew up. With its crispy texture and rich, spicy, molasses flavor, the cookie has always been one of my favorites. This recipe shares a similar flavor profile, with the addition of tender apples and fragrant orange blossom water. The result is a delicately perfumed and generously saucy dessert. During the summer months, I like to swap out the apples for peaches or nectarines. For a slightly less intense molasses flavor, use light brown sugar instead of dark. Serve the cobbler with vanilla ice cream.

topping

- 12 tablespoons (169 g) unsalted butter, plus more for the pan
- 1½ cups (180 g) all-purpose flour
- ¾ cup (161 g) packed dark brown sugar
- 1½ teaspoons baking powder
- ¾ teaspoon fine sea salt
- ⅓ cup (80 ml) whole milk

filling

- 3 medium Gala or Honeycrisp apples (514 g), peeled, cored, and cut into ¼-inch-thick (0.6 cm) slices
- 2 medium Granny Smith (or Honeycrisp) apples (342 g), peeled, cored, and cut into ¼-inch-thick (0.6 cm) slices
- ⅓ cup (72 g) packed dark brown sugar
- 2 tablespoons (30 g) fresh lemon juice
- 1 tablespoon all-purpose flour
- 1 tablespoon orange blossom water
- 1 teaspoon ground cinnamon
- ½ teaspoon ground ginger
- ¼ teaspoon fine sea salt

Vanilla ice cream for serving

1 Preheat the oven to 350°F (175°C). Grease an 8-inch square or 9-inch round baking dish.

2 *Make the brown butter for the topping*: Melt the butter in a small saucepan over medium heat, then continue to cook, swirling the pan occasionally, until it turns golden brown and develops a nutty aroma, 5 to 7 minutes; be careful not to let it burn. Remove from the heat and let cool.

3 *Make the filling*: Combine the apples, brown sugar, lemon juice, flour, orange blossom water, cinnamon, ginger, and salt in a large bowl and toss until the apples are evenly coated. Transfer the apple mixture to the prepared baking dish, spreading it out into an even layer.

4 *Make the topping*: Whisk together the flour, brown sugar, baking powder, and salt in a large bowl until thoroughly combined. Add the browned butter and mix with the dry ingredients using a rubber spatula. Add the milk and stir until the mixture comes together into a uniform dough. Drop spoonfuls of the topping mixture over the filling and spread evenly with the spatula.

5 Transfer the baking dish to the oven and bake for 40 to 45 minutes, until the topping feels springy to the touch and a toothpick inserted in the center comes out with just a few small, moist crumbs. Remove the cobbler from the oven and let cool for at least 15 minutes.

6 Serve the cobbler warm, with vanilla ice cream.

orange blossom lemon bars with mint sugar

makes 9 bars

Of the five basic tastes—salty, sweet, sour, bitter, and umami—sour is my favorite one by far. I often finish my dishes with a touch of acidity, like a squeeze of lemon, a dollop of cooling yogurt, or a vinegary salsa. When it comes to sweet treats, these lemon bars are what my sour dessert dreams are made of. They have a generous crust-to-filling ratio, with a creamy lemon curd filling that is subtly floral and pleasingly tart. Unlike most recipes for lemon bars, which call for first cooking the curd on the stovetop, here you just whisk all the ingredients together, spread the curd over the crust, and bake. You might be tempted to skip the mint sugar, but it adds a cooling and sweet kick that will make you think of a Moroccan version of a lemon mojito.

crust

- 9 tablespoons (127 g) unsalted butter, melted
- ⅓ cup (66 g) granulated sugar
- 1 teaspoon vanilla extract
- ¼ teaspoon fine sea salt
- 1½ cups (180 g) all-purpose flour

lemon curd

- 1¼ cups (250 g) granulated sugar
- Grated zest of 5 lemons (1 packed tablespoon)
- ⅓ cup (40 g) all-purpose flour
- ⅔ cup (160 g) fresh lemon juice
- 3 large eggs
- 1 tablespoon orange blossom water

mint sugar

- ¼ cup (50 g) granulated sugar
- ¼ cup (10 g) tightly packed mint leaves

1 Preheat the oven to 350°F (175°C). Line an 8-inch (20 cm) square baking pan with parchment paper, leaving an overhang on two opposite sides for easy removal of the bars.

2 *Make the crust*: Combine the melted butter, sugar, vanilla, and salt in a medium bowl. Add the flour and mix until a smooth dough forms. Transfer the dough to the prepared pan and use your hands to press it evenly over the bottom of the pan. Bake for 22 to 27 minutes, until the dough starts to firm up and the edges are lightly golden.

3 Remove the pan from the oven and use a fork to poke holes all over the crust (about 16 pokes), without going all the way down to the bottom of the pan.

4 *Meanwhile, make the lemon curd topping*: Combine the sugar and lemon zest in a large bowl and use your fingertips to rub them together until fragrant; this will help release the essential oils from the lemon zest and infuse the sugar with lemon flavor. Add the flour and stir to combine, then whisk in the lemon juice, eggs, and orange blossom water until well combined.

(recipe continues)

5 When the crust is ready, give the lemon curd a good stir to make sure it's thoroughly combined, and immediately pour it over the crust. Make sure to fill the pan with the lemon curd immediately after the crust is ready. If the crust cools, it will shrink and the curd will seep underneath.

6 Return the pan to the oven and bake for 22 to 27 minutes longer, until the lemon curd is just set in the center—not rubbery, and not excessively jiggly. Gently shake the pan; if the center of the filling barely jiggles, the lemon bars are ready. Remove from the oven and let cool completely.

7 Once the lemon bars have cooled, refrigerate for at least 2 hours, or overnight, to firm up the filling.

8 *Make the mint sugar*: Combine the sugar and mint in a small food processor or coffee or spice grinder and process until the mint is finely ground. Transfer to a small bowl and set aside. *(The mint sugar can be made ahead and refrigerated in a sealed container for up to 2 days.)*

9 Use a sharp knife to slice the lemon bars, sprinkle the mint sugar over them, and serve.

lemon and almond meskouta

makes 1 loaf cake

Meskouta is a beloved loaf cake commonly served at teatime in Morocco, known as "goûter" (from the French, meaning "snack" or "taste"). When I was younger, during my visits to my aunt's house every summer, this was my favorite time of day. The goûter table was filled with small savory and sweet treats, and there would always be a meskouta. Usually made with yogurt, oil, and orange juice, it's a simple snacking cake with a moist crumb and golden top that comes together quickly. This lemon-and-almond version is a delicious twist on the classic recipe, with a sweet lemon fragrance and a subtle hint of almond. It pairs perfectly with a refreshing glass of Moroccan mint tea.

- ¼ cup (25 g) sliced almonds
- ½ cup (120 g) olive oil, plus more for the pan
- 1½ cups (180 g) all-purpose flour
- ½ cup (60 g) almond flour
- 2 teaspoons baking powder
- ½ teaspoon baking soda
- ¾ teaspoon fine sea salt
- ¾ cup (150 g) granulated sugar
- Grated zest of 3 lemons (1½ packed teaspoons)
- 2 large eggs
- ¾ cup (180 g) Greek yogurt
- 3 tablespoons (45 g) fresh lemon juice
- 1 teaspoon vanilla extract

glaze

- 1 cup (120g) confectioners' sugar
- 1 tablespoon fresh lemon juice, plus more if necessary

1 Preheat the oven to 350°F (175°C). Spread the sliced almonds in a single layer on a small baking sheet and toast in the oven for 8 to 10 minutes, stirring the almonds or gently shaking the baking sheet halfway through for even toasting, until golden. Remove from the oven and set aside; leave the oven on. *(You can toast the almonds up to 3 days in advance and keep them in an airtight container.)*

2 Grease a 9-×-5-inch (22 × 12.7 cm) loaf pan with olive oil and line it with parchment paper, leaving an overhang on the two long sides for easy removal of the cake.

3 Whisk together the flour, almond flour, baking powder, baking soda, and salt in a medium bowl.

4 Combine the granulated sugar and lemon zest in a large bowl and use your fingertips to rub the sugar and lemon zest together until fragrant; this will help release the essential oils from the lemon zest and infuse the sugar with lemon flavor. Add the olive oil, eggs, yogurt, lemon juice, and vanilla extract and whisk until well combined. Add the dry ingredients and use a rubber spatula to mix just until you no longer see flecks of flour; make sure not to overmix the batter.

5 Transfer the batter to the prepared pan and use a spatula to spread it evenly. Bake the cake for 45 to 50 minutes, or until a toothpick inserted in the center comes out with some small, moist crumbs clinging to it. If the cake starts to brown too much before it is done, tent it loosely with foil. Remove the pan from the oven and allow the cake to cool completely on a wire rack.

6 *Make the glaze*: Combine the confectioners' sugar and lemon juice in a medium bowl and whisk together to obtain a smooth, thick glaze. If necessary, add more lemon juice ½ teaspoon at a time to make a pourable glaze.

7 Remove the cake from the pan, using the parchment overhang to help you, and transfer to a serving plate. Pour the glaze over the top of the cooled cake and garnish with the toasted almond slices.

ras el hanout chocolate chip banana bread

makes 1 loaf cake

I used to have a strong dislike of bananas until I tried a slice of banana-and-walnut bread from a small American coffee shop in Paris. The idea of baking bananas was a revelation to me; it made their flavor more nuanced and transformed their texture. In my Moroccan banana bread, the boldness of the dark chocolate and the sweetness of the bananas are balanced by the warm spices of the ras el hanout.

- 8 tablespoons (113 g) unsalted butter, melted and cooled, plus butter for the pan
- 1⅔ cups (200 g) all-purpose flour
- 1 teaspoon baking soda
- 1½ teaspoons baking powder
- 2 teaspoons ras el hanout, preferably homemade (page 38)
- ½ teaspoon ground cinnamon
- ½ teaspoon fine sea salt
- ⅔ cup (133 g) granulated sugar
- 2 large eggs
- 1 cup (230 g) mashed bananas (2 to 3 ripe bananas)
- 1½ teaspoons vanilla extract
- ⅔ cup (113 g) dark chocolate chips

1 Preheat the oven to 350°F (175°C). Grease a 9-×-5-inch (22.8 × 12.7 cm) loaf pan with butter and line it with parchment paper, leaving an overhang on the two long sides to make it easy to lift the loaf out of the pan.

2 Combine the flour, baking soda, baking powder, ras el hanout, cinnamon, and salt in a medium bowl and whisk to combine.

3 Whisk together the sugar and eggs in a large bowl until well combined. Add the mashed bananas, melted butter, and vanilla and whisk to combine. Add the dry ingredients and fold them in with a rubber spatula until you no longer see specks of flour; make sure not to overmix the batter, or the bread will be dense. Stir in the chocolate chips and mix just until incorporated.

4 Transfer the batter to the prepared pan and smooth the top with a rubber spatula. Bake the bread for 45 to 50 minutes, or until a toothpick inserted in the center comes out with only some small moist crumbs. If the bread starts to brown too much before it is baked, tent it loosely with foil.

5 Transfer the pan to a wire rack and allow to cool completely, then use the parchment overhang to remove the banana bread from the pan.

spiced affogato

serves 4

Because the country is so well known for its refreshing mint tea, many people are surprised to find out that Moroccans drink a lot of coffee. Moroccan spiced coffee is made with ground coffee beans brewed with a fragrant blend of spices. It is is usually prepared at home, rather than served in coffee shops and restaurants, so visitors often miss out on the opportunity to discover it. Like other Moroccan spice blends, the one used for this coffee tends to vary; some mixtures include saffron, nutmeg, and even dried rose petals. I will never forget a mix that that was sent to me from Ouarzazate, a southern city in the High Atlas Mountains, which contained more than forty different spices. For this spiced affogato, though, I chose to flavor my espresso shots with cinnamon, cardamom, ground ginger, and nutmeg, common spices used for coffee in Morocco. I think an affogato is one of the best ways to end a meal, with the sharpness of the espresso against the creamy sweetness of the gelato.

Ground coffee beans for 4 espresso shots (28 g)
¾ teaspoon ground cinnamon
¼ teaspoon freshly ground green cardamom (from the seeds of 6 to 9 pods)
¼ teaspoon gound ginger
4 gratings fresh nutmeg
4 scoops vanilla gelato or ice cream
Grated chocolate for garnish (optional)

1 Fill your espresso machine with the ground coffee. Transfer the cinnamon, cardamom, ginger and nutmeg to a large cup and brew 4 espresso shots directly into the cup. Stir the spices for a couple of minutes; this will help infuse the espresso with the spices.

2 Divide the espresso into four small cups or glasses, drop a scoop of ice cream or gelato into each cup or glass, garnish with grated chocolate, if using, and serve immediately.

amlou cinnamon knots

makes 12 knots

Something special happens when cinnamon and puff pastry come together; it's like culinary alchemy when the warm spice meets the buttery pastry. And these knots are extra special because they include amlou, often called "Moroccan Nutella," a Moroccan paste traditionally made with roasted almond butter, honey, and argan oil. The amlou in this recipe is slightly thicker than the traditional version (see Almond, Honey, and Argan Oil Paste—Amlou, page 49) so it can be used to fill the knots without running out of the rolls during baking.

I love this recipe because it calls for just a handful of ingredients, including store-bought puff pastry, which makes the preparation process much faster. And you can even shape the knots ahead and refrigerate them overnight before baking. This is a recipe to make when you have friends visiting and want to impress them with something familiar yet new. Serve these knots for breakfast or teatime.

amlou

- ½ cup (120 g) natural (ideally, roasted) almond butter, or substitute peanut butter
- 1½ tablespoons (33 g) honey
- 1 tablespoon argan oil, or substitute walnut or peanut oil
- ¼ teaspoon fine sea salt

- 2 sheets puff pastry, such as Dufour (about 14 ounces/396 g each)
- 1 large egg, beaten
- ½ cup (100 g) granulated sugar
- ¾ teaspoon ground cinnamon

1 *Make the amlou*: Combine the almond or peanut butter, honey, argan or nut oil, and salt in a medium bowl and stir together until smooth and well blended.

2 Unfold one of the puff pastry sheets on a lightly floured work surface or a sheet of parchment paper. Use the back of a large spoon or an offset spatula to spread the amlou over the sheet in a thin even layer, about ⅛ inch (0.3 cm) thick. The layer shouldn't be thicker than a coin; if it looks as if you will have excess amlou paste (your yield for the amlou may depend on the type of almond butter you are using), save the remainder for another use, as too much amlou will leak out when you slice the filled pastry.

3 Place the second puff pastry sheet on top of the first one, making sure that the edges of the sheets are aligned. Use a pizza cutter or sharp knife to cut the pastry rectangle lengthwise into 1-inch-wide (2.5 cm) strips.

(recipe continues)

4 Line two baking sheets with parchment paper. Pick up one pastry strip and shape it into a knot: Hold the opposite ends of the strip, pull on them slightly, then roll it up into a spiral and tuck the end of the strip into the center of the knot. Place the knot on one of the prepared sheets and continue shaping the knots, dividing them between the two sheets and leaving about 2 inches (5 cm) of space between them.

5 Cover the pastry knots and transfer to the fridge. Let rest for at least 45 minutes, and as long as overnight.

6 Preheat the oven to 400°F (205°C), with the racks in the upper and lower thirds. Brush the knots with the beaten egg and transfer to the oven. Bake for 30 to 35 minutes, switching the positions of the pans about halfway through, until the knots are puffed up and golden.

7 Meanwhile, combine the sugar and cinnamon in a medium bowl.

8 Remove the knots from the oven and let cool on the baking sheets for 1 to 2 minutes. Gently transfer each knot to the bowl of cinnamon sugar and turn to coat thoroughly with the sugar, then transfer to a plate.

9 Serve the knots warm or at room temperature. Leftovers will keep in a sealed container for up to 3 days.

nutella ghriba

makes 20 cookies

If you had asked my seven-year-old self what my dream cookie was, the answer would probably have been Nutella ghriba. I have always been a big chocolate lover, and, like much of the world's population, I love it paired with hazelnuts. Ghriba are Moroccan crinkled cookies that are usually made with almonds or walnuts. You'll often see them elegantly displayed in bakery cases or in the souk, adorned with a generous dusting of powdered sugar. These chocolate-hazelnut ghriba are as delicious as they are fun to make, and they boast an irresistible, soft, melt-in-your-mouth texture.

- 1⅓ cups (186 g) blanched hazelnuts
- 1 cup (120 g) all-purpose flour
- 3 tablespoons (24 g) unsweetened cocoa powder
- 1 teaspoon baking powder
- ½ teaspoon fine sea salt
- 7 ounces (200 g) semisweet chocolate, finely chopped
- 4 tablespoons (60 g) unsalted butter, cut into pieces
- ½ cup (100 g) granulated sugar
- 2 large eggs
- 1 cup (120 g) confectioners' sugar

1 Preheat the oven to 350°F (175°C). Spread the hazelnuts on a rimmed baking sheet and toast in the oven for 10 to 15 minutes, until golden; shake the pan halfway through for even browning. Remove from the oven and let cool to room temperature.

2 Transfer the hazelnuts to a food processor and pulse until finely ground, stopping occasionally to scrape down the sides of the bowl for even blending; be careful not to overprocess the nuts, or they may turn into hazelnut butter.

3 Transfer the ground nuts to a large bowl and add the flour, cocoa powder, baking powder, and salt. Use a whisk or a fork to mix until thoroughly combined. Set aside.

4 Put the chocolate and butter in a microwave-safe bowl and microwave for 15-second intervals, stirring after each one, until melted and smooth. Set aside.

5 Combine the granulated sugar and eggs in a medium bowl and stir with a fork or a whisk until smooth and well blended. Add the melted chocolate mixture and stir until well combined and smooth.

(recipe continues)

6 Add the egg and chocolate mixture to the dry ingredients and stir with a large spoon or rubber spatula until all of it is thoroughly incorporated. Cover and refrigerate for at least 2 hours, or as long as overnight. If refrigerated for more than 4 hours, the dough might become too firm; if that's the case, let it stand at room temperature for 30 minutes.

7 Preheat the oven to 350°F (175°C), with the racks in the upper and lower thirds. Line 2 baking sheets with parchment paper. Put the confectioners' sugar in a small shallow bowl.

8 Scoop up about 1½ tablespoons (34 g) of dough for each cookie and shape into a ball (a bit smaller than a golf ball), then roll several times in confectioners' sugar, until generously coated, and transfer to one of the prepared sheet pans; leave at least 2 inches (5 cm) between the cookies.

9 Lightly press each cookie with your fingertips to flatten it slightly. Place in the oven and bake, rotating the pans and switching them between the racks halfway through, for 10 to 13 minutes, or until the cookies are cracked, the edges appear set, and the centers are still soft. Remove from the oven and allow the cookies to cool on the pans for 15 minutes to firm up, then transfer to a wire rack to cool completely.

10 The cookies can be stored in an airtight container at room temperature for up to 5 days.

TIP: If blanched hazelnuts are not available, you can remove the skins by blanching the nuts in boiling water. Put the hazelnuts in a medium pot or saucepan and add enough water to fully submerge them. Bring the water to a boil over medium-high heat and blanch the nuts for 3 minutes. To test the nuts, use a slotted spoon to remove one nut from the pot and run it under cold water (or use an ice bath) until cool enough to handle, then check to see if the skin comes off easily. If it does not, boil for another minute or two and test again. Once the hazelnuts are ready, drain them in a colander and run under cold water until cool, then drain again. Once they have cooled, gently rub the hazelnuts between your hands or in a clean kitchen towel to remove the skins; it's totally fine if some skins remain.

almond macaroons

makes 18 cookies

These macaroons, known as "maalka," which means "chewy" in Moroccan Arabic, are a popular treat sold in the vibrant streets of the souks. They have a satisfying texture and carry notes of caramel, almond, and orange blossom. Whenever I bake them, I am impressed once again by how simple they are to prepare and how few ingredients they require, but you do need to plan ahead; the dough has to rest for at least 12 hours to achieve its distinct flavor and texture. For this recipe, I recommend using a scale for measuring, especially to weigh the egg whites, to ensure the proper ingredient ratios.

- 1⅔ cups (238 g) unblanched (skin-on) raw almonds, plus 18 almonds for garnish
- 1⅓ cups (160 g) confectioners' sugar
- 2 large egg whites (2.4 ounces/67 g) from very fresh eggs
- 2 teaspoons orange blossom water
- Generous pinch of ground cinnamon
- ¼ teaspoon fine sea salt

1 Pulse the almonds in a food processor until finely ground and powdery, stopping occasionally to scrape down the sides of the bowl for even blending; this may take a couple of minutes. Be careful not to overprocess the almonds, or they will turn into almond butter.

2 Transfer the ground almonds to a large bowl and add the confectioners' sugar, egg whites, orange blossom water, cinnamon, and salt. Use a rubber spatula or a large spoon to blend the ingredients well. Cover with plastic wrap or transfer to a container with a tight-fitting lid and refrigerate for at least 12 hours, and up to 48 hours, to firm up the dough.

3 Preheat the oven to 350°F (175°C), with the racks in the upper and lower thirds. Line two baking sheets with parchment paper.

4 Scoop up 1 rounded tablespoon (30 g) of dough for each cookie, shape into a ball (a bit smaller than a golf ball), and transfer to one of the prepared sheet pans, leaving at least 3 inches (7.6 cm) between the cookies. If the dough is very sticky, lightly moisten your hands to shape the cookies. Place an almond in the center of each dough ball and use your fingertips to lightly press it into the cookie; this will also flatten it slightly.

5 Bake for 12 to 15 minutes, rotating the pans and switching them between the racks halfway through, until the cookies are golden, the edges appear set, and the centers are still soft. Remove from the oven and allow the cookies to cool on the pans for 15 minutes to firm up, then transfer to a wire rack to cool completely.

6 The cookies can be stored in an airtight container at room temperature for up to 5 days.

TIP: You can use the leftover egg yolks to make Pistachio Jawhara Cups (page 243).

ACKNOWLEDGMENTS

Madaq began as a small seed I planted in my mind in early 2019, one that quietly took root and stayed with me. Bringing it to life—and finally into your hands—took time, dedication, and patience. While I'll admit patience isn't my forte, I'm grateful for those years in between. They allowed me to grow not just as a cook but as also as a person—making this book as special as I had envisioned.

First and foremost, my deepest gratitude goes to Dan Halpern for believing in my vision and giving me the freedom to produce the book I truly wanted to create and write. Your support and guidance have been invaluable.

Writing a book takes a village, and I am beyond grateful for mine:

Ben Clark, my literary agent—thank you for believing in *Madaq,* for helping me refine my blurry ideas into something tangible, and for your keen insights in shaping its identity.

Judith Sutton—for your thoughtful guidance and meticulous editing. Your expertise elevated this book in ways I deeply appreciate.

Lisa Nicklin—for your dedication, enthusiasm, and culinary expertise. Your feedback and suggestions made the recipe testing smoother, and far less stressful.

Jinane Ennasri—thank you for embarking on this intense road trip and photo shoot with me. The way you see and love Morocco made this book all the more special. I'm grateful for your talent.

Issy Crocker—for your ability to take effortlessly beautiful pictures, your creativity, and your precision.

My favorite food styling duo, led by Emily Ezekiel with Joseph Denison Carey—thank you for showing up, cooking up a storm, and making me smile, and even laugh, along the way. I wish we could do it all over again.

The design team, led by Deb Wood, with Isa Connolly and Blair Kelly—thank you for transforming my chaotic mood board into something beautifully realized. Your patience and artistry brought *Madaq* to life in ways I could have only hoped for.

Lexy Bloom—for your brilliant editorial expertise, patience, and support throughout the whole process.

Rob Shapiro—for handling all the behind-the-scenes coordination with patience and kindness.

My mom—for continuously teaching me the basics of Moroccan food and always picking up the phone when I have a question.

To the rest of my family and my friends—thank you for your unwavering support, and for all the times I couldn't show up because I was knee-deep in recipe writing or testing. Your love and belief in me fuelled this project.

An extra-special thanks to Zayd, my husband—for being my rock, my home, and my guiding light.

And finally, to you—my readers, supporters, and fellow lovers of Moroccan food. Thank you for following along, cooking my recipes, and coming to my events and restaurant, and for every kind note you've sent my way. You inspire me to keep sharing my passion for Moroccan cuisine. This book is for you.

8

INDEX

Page numbers in *italics* refer to illustrations.

A

B

C

D

E

A NOTE ON THE TYPE

This book features Avenir, a beautifully crafted sans serif typeface designed by Adrian Frutiger (1928–2015) and released by Linotype in 1988. Avenir blends traditional twentieth-century geometric forms with humanist design principles, achieving a harmonious balance between circular and rectilinear elements. Its subtle stroke modulation enhances both legibility and warmth.

Composed by North Market Street Graphics,
Lancaster, Pennsylvania

Designed by Deb Wood